EXPLORATIONS IN ECCLESIOLOGY AND ETHNOGRAPHY

STUDIES IN ECCLESIOLOGY AND ETHNOGRAPHY

Series Editors

Pete Ward, Christian Scharen, Paul Fiddes, John Swinton, and James Nieman

The STUDIES IN ECCLESIOLOGY AND ETHNOGRAPHY series is focused on the development of new forms of cross-disciplinary scholarship in the study of the Church. The series has grown out of a convergence around the attempt to rethink the customary divide between empirical and theological analyses of the Church within Religious Studies, Systematic Theology, and Practical Theology. The volumes in the series will explore methodological and substantive issues that arise from theological and empirical studies of the practices and social reality of the Church. Ethnography is defined by the series editors "inclusively" as any form of qualitative research. The series will include both multi-author volumes and monographs.

PUBLISHED VOLUMES

Explorations in Ecclesiology and Ethnography
   Christian B. Scharen, Editor

Perspectives on Ecclesiology and Ethnography
   Pete Ward, Editor

Explorations in Ecclesiology and Ethnography

Edited by

Christian B. Scharen

WILLIAM B. EERDMANS PUBLISHING COMPANY

GRAND RAPIDS, MICHIGAN / CAMBRIDGE, U.K.

© 2012 Christian B. Scharen

Published 2012 by
Wm. B. Eerdmans Publishing Co.
2140 Oak Industrial Drive N.E., Grand Rapids, Michigan 49505 /
P.O. Box 163, Cambridge CB3 9PU U.K.

Printed in the United States of America

17 16 15 14 13 12   7 6 5 4 3 2 1

Library of Congress Cataloging-in-Publication Data

Explorations in ecclesiology and ethnography / edited by Christian B. Scharen.
        p.   cm.   — (Studies in ecclesiology and ethnography)
    Includes bibliographical references and index.
    ISBN 978-0-8028-6864-0 (pbk.: alk. paper)
    1. Church.   2. Ethnography — Religious aspects — Christianity.
    I. Scharen, Christian Batalden.

    BV600.3.E97   2012
    262 — dc23

                                                    2012018157

www.eerdmans.com

Contents

PART THREE: ON CONGREGATIONS AND SOCIETY

Contributors

CHRISTOPHER CRAIG BRITTAIN, Senior Lecturer in Practical Theology, University of Aberdeen

HELEN CAMERON, Director of Research at Ripon College Cuddesdon

HENK DE ROEST, Professor of Practical Theology, Protestant Theological University, The Netherlands

PAUL S. FIDDES, Professor of Systematic Theology, University of Oxford

MATHEW GUEST, Lecturer in Sociology of Religion, Department of Theology and Religion, Durham University

ROGER HAIGHT, SJ, Scholar in Residence, Union Theological Seminary

HARALD HEGSTAD, Professor of Systematic Theology, Norwegian School of Theology, Oslo, Norway

MARK T. MULDER, Associate Professor, Sociology, Calvin College

PAUL D. MURRAY, Professor of Systematic Theology, Department of Theology and Religion, Durham University

JAMES NIEMAN, Professor of Practical Theology, Hartford Seminary

CHRISTIAN B. SCHAREN, Teaches worship and practical theology at Luther Seminary and is co-investigator of the *Learning Pastoral Imagination Project*

James K. A. Smith, Professor of Philosophy, Calvin College

Pete Ward, Senior Lecturer in Youth Ministry and Theological Education, King's College, London

Clare Watkins, Teaches Pastoral Theology at Westminster Seminary and is a member of the research project, *Action Research — Church and Society*

Introduction
Christian B. Scharen

Congregations' central purpose is of course the expression and trans-
mission of religious meaning, and corporate worship is the primary way
in which that purpose is pursued.

Mark Chaves, *Congregations in America*

Through liturgy we are shaped to live rightly the story of God, to be-
come part of that story, and are thus able to recognize and respond to
the saints in our midst.

Stanley Hauerwas, *Christian Existence Today*

To a Christian pastoral leader who regularly plans and leads worship, or to
the Christian congregational member who regularly participates in worship, neither of these quotes rings true as a description of what happens in
church. Each is too formal in its own way. One is descriptive, using an analytic or scientific language quite distant from the self-understandings of
worshipers themselves. To be fair, Chaves's analytic language does not
mean to describe the worshipers' self-understandings; it means to "explain" to other scientists what they are doing. Hauerwas, a Christian theologian, comes no closer with his normative language, drawing as he does
from multiple theological traditions (narrative, virtue) that are again quite
distant from the variable actual self-understandings of worshipers. Research and writing on the church, then, suffers as a result of these separate

1

and deeply rutted paths upon which careers run. The mission of God in and through the church and its pastoral leadership suffers as a result, insofar as this divide keeps scholarship from understanding the actual lived experience of the church. The proposal of the series to which this volume belongs is that in order for scholarship about the church to be most helpful to the church — gathered in community and scattered in daily life — rapprochement between empirical and theological understandings of the church ought to be encouraged in such a way that the actual life of the church is attended to, thought through theologically, and thereby strengthened (one hopes) for more faithful witness.

Overcoming this divide is a major personal pastoral and scholarly aim of mine. As I moved through seminary training and early pastoral leadership experiences in congregations, I felt the yawning gap between the formal historical and systematic theology I learned in classes and the actual reality of the church as I experienced it. Unable at that time to find congregational studies courses in seminary, I studied sociology of religion with Robert Bellah across the street from Pacific Lutheran Theological Seminary at the University of California Berkeley. Tutored under his deeply normative vision for sociology of religion, and his explicit efforts to seek rapprochement between theology and social science, I found a major source of help for understanding the life of the church and the pastoral leadership needed to foster vibrant and faithful ministry within it.[1]

This deep passion led me to do doctoral studies at Emory University, where I combined pastoral work at a small congregation in East Point, Georgia, with nearly three years of fieldwork in five different congregations in the Atlanta Metro area. In carrying out this ethnographic research, I found strong encouragement to seek ways to explicitly hold theology and social science together as a means to better understand the life of the church and, especially, its pastoral leaders. In the decade since, partly spent in parish ministry and partly spent teaching in the academy, I have sought out partners with whom to mine the riches found at this intersection of ethnography and ecclesiology.

The proposal behind this book, then, along with its partner volume in the series (*Perspectives on Ecclesiology and Ethnography,* edited by Pete Ward), contends that in order for scholarship *about* the church to be most helpful *to* the church's missional engagement in daily life, both through its

---

1. Robert N. Bellah and Steven M. Tipton, *The Robert Bellah Reader* (Durham, NC: Duke University Press, 2006), esp. part four, "Sociology and Theology," pp. 451-552.

pastoral leadership and its living corporate membership as the body of Christ, rapprochement between empirical and theological understandings of the church ought to be encouraged. This volume both follows from, and in some sense depends upon, the first volume in the series. Readers are encouraged to seek out that volume as well, for although this volume can be engaged on its own, it only summarizes the much more fully elaborated arguments to be found there. These initial volumes in the Ecclesiology and Ethnography Series result from a series of initial conferences that have built a network of scholars and a research agenda drawing together those working empirically and theologically on the church for the sake of a third constituency. That third constituency is pastoral leadership and faithful church membership at a time of great upheaval and change in both church and society. The foundational aim of this work is to further turn scholarship to the task of strengthening pastoral leaders and the congregations they serve as they seek to understand and effectively guide congregations for the sake of faithful witness and service in the world.

Disciplinary Divides

These two areas or approaches for research on the church — ethnography, understood more generally as qualitative research, and ecclesiology, understood as normative theological research — have generally remained distinct and distinctive. This fact is as true in departments of religious studies at major universities as it is in small denominational seminaries. While there are many causes, the divide is a result of religious studies being broken into separate disciplines, and the tribalism that occurs among academic conferences. On the one hand, scholars have pursued empirical knowledge of the church — when they have pursued it at all — within a framework separate from the claims of faith. Even when carried out by people of faith, such analyses have largely been done by bracketing "personal faith" so as to be accepted as "objective" and therefore "true."

While many defenses of this sort of bracketing could be brought out as evidence, Peter Berger's attempt to maintain a "methodological atheism" in his works of sociology, as opposed to his more explicitly confessional works, stands out as an influential example.[2] While Berger's work is a generation old now, the quote from Mark Chaves at the outset of this in-

---

2. See especially Peter Berger, *The Sacred Canopy* (New York: Doubleday, 1967), p. 180.

troduction makes clear that such a perspective is far from passé in writing on the church today. Using a theoretical language surely foreign to the believer, Chaves proceeds to describe American congregational worship practices across almost forty pages of text in an effort to explain "the fascinating puzzle about the nature of change in collective religious practice."[3] When in such a text the language for description is merely academic and in service of explanation, one gets the distinct sense that the actual beliefs and practices of participants in congregational worship are not allowed to be true depictions of what is really going on.

Some theologians have critiqued the way such empirical research polices the boundaries of its work to keep out theological ideas.[4] They have, in response, sought to describe congregational worship in quite different terms. Yet they in their own way have dismissed or at least ignored actual congregations and the primary theology of the worshipers in favor of their own conversations with the great thinkers of the tradition and the present day. Furthermore, such theologians as Stanley Hauerwas (whom I quote above) and John Milbank, to name the most prominent, have explicitly dismissed social science as a defective means of learning about the church.[5] Instead they turn either to idealized understandings of the church or to "naïve descriptions" of actual congregational life with their own theological analysis spread over the top like thick jam.[6]

Recent work on the church has benefited from an effort to rethink the traditional divide between empirical, cultural, and theological analyses. Within ecclesiology there has been an emerging interest on the part of some to draw upon cultural theory as well as various understandings of a theory of practice(s).[7] While not always directly engaging with congrega-

---

3. Mark Chaves, *Congregations in America* (Cambridge, MA: Harvard University Press, 2004).

4. Here, see "Policing the Sublime: A Critique of the Sociology of Religion," chapter 5 in John Milbank, *Theology and Social Theory: Beyond Secular Reason* (Oxford: Blackwell, 1990), pp. 101-43.

5. Milbank, *Theology and Social Theory;* Stanley Hauerwas, *Christian Existence Today* (Grand Rapids: Brazos Press, 2001).

6. Stanley Hauerwas, *Sanctify Them in Truth: Holiness Exemplified* (Nashville: Abingdon, 1998), p. 160, note 8.

7. In addition to Hauerwas and Milbank, see Kathryn Tanner, *Theories of Culture* (Minneapolis: Fortress, 1997); as well as Nicholas Healy, "Practices and the New Ecclesiology: Misplaced Concreteness?" *International Journal of Systematic Theology* 5 (November 2003): 287-308; Christian Scharen, "'Judicious Narratives,' or Ethnography as Ecclesiology," *Scottish Journal of Theology* 58, no. 2 (2005): 125-42.

tions, on the whole such work has at least had the effect of raising the question, "Where is the church?"[8] Some scholars in theology, especially those working in what is broadly termed "practical theology," have shown an increasing interest in social science, and in ethnography in particular, as a means of gaining rich empirical data on particular churches as one part of their theological work proper.[9] At the same time, there has been a renewed wave of interest in the empirical study of the church.[10] A number of these studies draw explicitly on the tools of ethnography but with a distinctly theological openness that is rare in empirical research of any sort.[11]

Explorations of Congregations: Ecclesiology and Ethnography in Action

The chapters of this volume have been divided into three sections in part to clump them according to the ways they attend to the life of the church or perhaps better the modes of church to which they attend. The first section opens up our explorations with rich reflection on what is to be gained for our understanding of congregations when empirical and theological approaches work in a collaborative way. The rest of the volume unfolds

---

8. John Milbank, "Enclaves, or Where Is the Church?" *New Blackfriars* 73 (June 1992): 341-52.

9. Don Browning and Johannes van der Ven were leaders of this move in practical theology. See Browning, *A Fundamental Practical Theology* (Minneapolis: Fortress Press, 1991); and van der Ven, *Entwurf einer Empirischen Theologie* (Kampen: Kok; Weinheim: Deutscher Studienverlag, 1990). For one recent example of where this conversation has come, see Leslie J. Francis, Mandy Robbins, and Jeff Astley, eds., *Empirical Theology in Texts and Tables: Qualitative, Quantitative and Comparative Perspectives* (Leiden: Brill, 2009), representing the work of the International Society of Empirical Research in Theology.

10. In addition to Chaves, among many others, see Nancy Ammerman, *Pillars of Faith* (Berkeley: University of California Press, 2005); Penny Becker, *Congregations in Conflict* (New York: Cambridge University Press, 1999); Nancy Eiesland, *A Particular Place* (New Brunswick, NJ: Rutgers University Press, 2000); and, in the UK, Mathew Guest, Karen Tusting, and Linda Woodhead, *Congregational Studies in the UK: Christianity in a Post-Christian Context* (London: Ashgate, 2004).

11. Christian Scharen, *Public Worship, Public Work* (Collegeville, MN: Liturgical Press, 2004); Pete Ward, *Selling Worship* (London: Paternoster, 2005); James Steven, *Worship in the Spirit* (London: Paternoster, 2002); Ryan Bolger and Eddie Gibbs, *The Emerging Church* (Grand Rapids: Baker, 2006); Mark Gornik, *To Live in Peace* (Grand Rapids: Eerdmans, 2005); Mary McClintock Fulkerson, *Places of Redemption* (New York: Oxford University Press, 2008).

fruitful and wide-ranging discussions of such issues as geographic habits of evangelicals, debates over difficult issues like homosexuality, responses to social problems like drug abuse and homelessness, as well as baptism and Eucharist, here explored in direct engagement with congregational practice rather than the typical ideal mode of theological research that merely gestures toward normative practice in a generic way. As in the first volume in the series, we have not attempted to hold participants to a uniform line of argument but rather proposed a way of doing grounded theological work, "concrete ecclesiology" as Nicolas Healy has called it, and let the participants work with that conception as they see fit. The result is a provocative and heady brew that ought to stimulate further conversation, research, and writing, and, more important, will perhaps also inspire faithfulness in living church in the world today.

PART ONE

On Congregations and the Church

CHAPTER 1

On the Dynamic Relation between Ecclesiology and Congregational Studies

James Nieman and Roger Haight, SJ

Ecclesiology is presently responding to two sources of pressure from opposite directions. On the one hand, a more exact knowledge of the historical origins of the church and the variety of forms the church has assumed across its historical life challenge the idea of a normative ecclesiology. On the other hand, emergent churches in all parts of the world, particularly in Africa and Asia, sometimes appear to stand at the margins of being identifiably Christian. These two concerns intersect in the study of some congregations where broad doctrinal claims about the church are being tested by a realistic scrutiny of the concrete political and social dynamisms driving particular churches and the practices of actual congregations. Part of the liveliness of the discipline of ecclesiology today stems from an interaction between the desire to preserve the essential character of the church and the need that it adapt to new historical situations, between a normative con-

---

The co-authors are theologians of different denominations and different ecclesiological subdisciplines. Originally, parts 1 and 2 were developed in a dialogue between the authors for a 2007 Yale Divinity School conference titled "Ecclesiology and Ethnography: Exploring the Emerging Conversation Between Theology and Congregational Studies." The dialogue across denominational and disciplinary lines accounts for the authors' citations of each other's works. Because the papers converged, they are combined and offered under a single title. Roger Haight is mainly responsible for part 1 and James Nieman for part 2. This chapter first appeared as: Roger Haight and James Nieman, "On the Dynamic Relation Between Ecclesiology and Congregational Studies," *Theological Studies* 70 (2009): 577-99. Republished with the kind permission of the journal.

cept of the church and the need that it become inculturated in the life of its members.

The foci of these two pressure points are addressed by two distinct subdisciplines of ecclesiology, the one pursuing a normative concept of the church, the other studying its historical manifestations, most concretely in congregational studies. Taking up these lines of force, this chapter develops a response to the following questions: How does formal academic ecclesiology relate to congregational studies, and vice versa? The chapter contains two parts. The first assumes the point of view of academic ecclesiology, and from that perspective theorizes on the relationship between these two ecclesiological subdisciplines. The second assumes the perspective of the discipline of congregational studies and reflects on how that field of study bears on the more general understanding of the church as such. The two probes into this relationship yield remarkably similar conclusions concerning the mutual relevance and influence that each discipline should have on the other in advancing a more holistic understanding of church.

Part 1: From the Perspective of General Ecclesiology

We begin this analysis of the relationship between general or formal ecclesiology and congregational studies from the broader vantage point of the former as distinct from the particular focus of congregational studies.[1] This part is divided into three sections. The first establishes further the methodological presuppositions from which these ecclesiological reflections arise. From that basis it formulates an understanding of the relationship between general ecclesiology and congregational studies in four theses. The third section will then test those theses by entering into dialogue with an earlier writing of James Nieman on congregational studies and ecclesiology on the specific topic of the marks of the church.

---

1. That is, since the perspectives of the two authors are both "ecclesiological," no one term suffices to distinguish the breadth of the one field from the particularity of the other. For our purposes, "formal" or "academic" or "general" will be used to specify the broader field, however inadequate this designation may sometimes be.

Ecclesiology from Below

This first foray into ecclesiological language, especially regarding presuppositions and method, is designed to lay out some of the presuppositions and principles in the study of the church that govern part 1 of this chapter. Ecclesiological method and language are far from standardized. Thus we begin by mapping the field on which this particular game will be played. This may be accomplished by a contrast between ecclesiology from above and from below and a consideration of some of the consequences that flow from a method that proceeds from below.

The phrases "from above" and "from below" in ecclesiology operate by analogy with their use in Christology. The key word in both terms is "from"; the phrases designate a point of departure and a method, not content. Christology from above begins the process of understanding the person Jesus Christ with statements of authority that name the confessional beliefs of Christians about Jesus Christ; these may be drawn from Scripture or from the classical doctrines about Christ; they are metaphysical in character. By contrast, Christology from below begins the formal process of understanding and explaining who Jesus Christ is by first focusing on the appearance of Jesus of Nazareth in history and the religious experience of him that led to the doctrinal interpretations. Christology from below begins with history and traces the genesis and development of christological belief. Although the point of departure of this Christology is historical, it concludes with equally confessional interpretations of Jesus and hermeneutical appropriations of them. The result is critical affirmation of Jesus as the Christ in whom is found God's salvation.

The contrast in ecclesiology is analogous. In ecclesiology from above, understanding the church begins with and is based upon the authority of Scripture or classical doctrines. It usually presupposes a specific church. Its nature and qualities are characterized by biblical metaphors — "the body of Christ" is a good example. The origin of the church is construed in doctrinal terms with Jesus Christ as the founder, so that the ministries and corresponding structure of the church correlate with God's will. By contrast, ecclesiology from below begins historically with a historical account of the genesis of the church beginning with the ministry of Jesus. In a critical historical account, Jesus' role in the origin of the church is shifted from being founder to being the foundation of a church that comes into being later in the first century in the memory of Jesus and under the influence of the Spirit. Ecclesiology from below traces the gradual formation of the

11

church during the first century, using historical and sociological categories and also recognizing the early church's experience and testimony to the power of God in the whole movement, that is, its theological dimension. In contrast to the tendency of ecclesiology from above, ecclesiology from below notices the pluralism of church polities during the course of the church's formation.

Much more should be said about the qualities of these two types of ecclesiology, but the point here is simply to stipulate that this whole chapter unfolds within the framework of an ecclesiology from below. From the perspectives of both authors, this method offers a more adequate approach in our historically conscious and theologically critical age. On that premise, we can lay down at least two qualities of a historically conscious ecclesiology that will have a bearing on the subject matter of this chapter.

First, an ecclesiology from below not only begins with history but also continues to attend to the existential historical community that calls itself church. The historical point of departure also remains as the consistent referent of what is said about the church. We know nothing of a heavenly church before grasping the church of history. The shift to a historical genetic base or starting point for understanding the church widens the field of vision. A historically conscious ecclesiology from below has to attend to the whole Christian movement. Ecclesiology through the ages and in particular after the Reformation has become a tribal discipline: each church has its own ecclesiology; each finds its own polity reflected in the New Testament; and so on. Against this trend, ecclesiology from below imposes on the ecclesiologist what may be called a "whole-part" optic. One's own particular church is not the whole church, although the whole church in a theological sense is manifest in it; rather, the particular church is both authentic church and part of a larger embodiment of the church of which a single church is a part.[2]

A second quality of ecclesiology from below cautions against reductionism in a historical and sociological interpretation of the church. The data for ecclesiology include the empirical history of the genesis and development of the church and also the development of the beliefs of the

2. The word "church" is analogous because of the variety of its referents: the whole church, a denomination, a national or regional organization, a theological/juridical unit such as a diocese or synod, a parish or congregation. Generally it is apparent when "church" refers to the whole Christian movement. The context often makes it clear whether "particular church" refers to a denomination (Greek Orthodox, Presbyterian, etc.) or a congregation. Sometimes "particular church" can logically and meaningfully refer to both.

community about its nature and purpose. The church in its beginnings and constantly through its history bears witness to the presence and power of God in its origins, development, religious life, and future. It lives in and by the power of Christ and the Holy Spirit as the source of the transcendent energy that brought it into being and, as promise, sustains its life into the future. There can be no historicist or sociological reduction of the church in an ecclesiology from below to a merely human organization. The historical data include the confessional witness to a transcendent dimension of the church.

Four Theses on the Relation of General Ecclesiology and Congregational Studies

From the basis of an ecclesiology from below, we can now move to four theses that together broadly define the disciplinary relationship between general ecclesiology and the more focused discipline of congregational studies. The first thesis governs the others: it posits that the study of the church has to be simultaneously historical and theological. From this thesis flow the next three theses, which move in the following direction: on the supposition that the basic unit of the church is the congregation, one can say, broadly speaking, that congregational studies determine the object of ecclesiology. Even so, formal ecclesiology, appealing to theological data, determines the nature and purpose of this social institution. However, the normative theological claims about the church are chastened and measured by congregational studies. The relationship is thus interactive and dynamic.[3]

1. *The study of the church must attend simultaneously to the historical and theological character of the church.* A very first principle of ecclesiology deserving attention states that the church exists in a twofold relationship: it is simultaneously related to the world and to God. Because of this duality, the church must always be understood simultaneously in two languages: concrete historical language and theological language, sociological language and doctrinal language.[4] With a moment's reflection it becomes

3. The use of theses in this exposition allows a succinct statement of a position that, of course, needs to be further nuanced and thus invites dialogue. Confines of space also explain the terse didactic style of this chapter.

4. The phrase indicating that the church is one reality described in two languages is drawn from Edward Schillebeeckx, *Church: The Human Story of God* (New York: Crossroad,

self-evident that the church exists in a twofold relationship to the world and to God. The point of making the distinction, then, lies in the attention it focuses on the difference between these relationships so that we can see clearly how they relate to each other. The two relationships coexist and mutually influence and condition each other. This has first of all a bearing on how we understand the church, both generally and at any given time and in any particular instance. On the one hand, the church cannot be understood exclusively in theological terms; on the other, it cannot be understood in exclusively empirical, historical, or worldly terms. The principle forbids any reductionist understanding of the church in either direction.[5] Schleiermacher expresses the tension for understanding the church this way: a merely theological interpretation of the church would be empty and unreal; a merely historical interpretation of the church would miss completely its inner reality or substance.[6]

The twofold relationship that constitutes the church means that two sources of energy flow into the church, one coming from the world, the other coming from God. The twofold relationship to the world and to God

---

1990), pp. 210-13. He writes: "The church community as mystery cannot be found behind or above concrete, visible reality. The church community is to be found in this reality which can be demonstrated here and now" (p. 213). The divine and human dimensions of the church are like divine grace and human freedom: when they are related conceptually, they are "thought of as being next to and alongside each other, but in truth they are one and the same thing, a text to be deciphered in different language games" (p. 212).

5. James Gustafson defines theological reductionism in this way: "By theological reductionism we mean the exclusive use of Biblical and doctrinal language in the interpretation of the church" (James M. Gustafson, *Treasure in Earthen Vessels: The Church as a Human Community* [New York: Harper & Brothers, 1961; Chicago: University of Chicago Press, 1976], p. 100). By contrast, historical and social reductionism would mean the exclusive use of social-historical language in the interpretation of the church. The key word in both is "exclusive."

6. Schleiermacher expresses this principle in terms of abstract invariant qualities in the church and changeable features: "If the attempt were made to set forth the self-identical and invariable element in Christianity in complete abstraction from the historical, it would scarcely be distinguishable from the undertaking of people who imagine that they are expounding Christianity when in point of fact what they offer is pure speculation. And if anyone tried to present solely the variable in Christian history in complete abstraction from the self-identical, his aim would apparently be the same as that of people who, penetrating no further than the outer husk of things, permit us to see in the history of the Church nothing but the complex and pernicious play of blinded passion" (Friedrich Schleiermacher, *The Christian Faith*, ed. H. R. Mackintosh and J. S. Stewart [New York: Harper & Row, 1963], § 126, p. 585).

should not be conceived as defining a stable state, passive and inert. The duality points to a dynamic interaction of nature and grace. The relationship of the church to God marks a line of power within the lives of the people who constitute the church and through them to the wider community itself. The same is true of the relationship to the world. Schleiermacher also describes these two interacting forces in the church with the perhaps misleading language of the "invisible" and "visible" church. He writes, "Thus the invisible church is the totality of the effects of the Spirit as a connected whole; but these effects, as connected with those lingering influences of the collective life of universal sinfulness which are never absent from any life that has been taken possession of by the divine Spirit, constitute the visible church."[7] But the visible aspect of the church should not be reduced to or equated with what is sinful. It includes the whole positive dynamics of history, society, and institution.

Schleiermacher is close to Schillebeeckx on this point. There is only one church, and it is an empirical, historical phenomenon. The Spirit of God released by Jesus the Christ is at work in this church, however, and the activity of God as Spirit sets up a tension between the drag of the sinfulness of the world within the church and the uplifting and divinizing effects of the Spirit. The term "invisible church" refers to all those effects, the sum total of them, that flow from God as Spirit. This distinction underscores that the church can never be reduced to a human organization and never romanticized with a theological language that leaves the organization behind. It also represents these two sides of the church as a dynamic interaction of forces. On the personal level, God's Spirit or grace moves to open up the lethargic and egoistic dimensions of human freedom into self-transcendence and service of the other. On the social level, as water becomes sign or symbol of God's action within human existence in baptism, so too the social-historical and institutional aspects of the church, which often appear to limit human freedom and confine the Spirit, can be transformed into platforms for genuine spiritual activity. According to the principles of sacramentality and accommodation, God acts in the world through creatures, human agents, and institutions.[8]

We began by distinguishing between ecclesiology from above and from below in order to clarify a perspective. The strategy is to distinguish

---

7. Schleiermacher, *The Christian Faith*, § 148, p. 677.

8. See John Calvin, *Institutes of the Christian Religion*, ed. John T. McNeill (Philadelphia: Westminster, 1960), 4.3.1 (pp. 1053-54).

in order to unite elements coherently. These principles put these aspects of the church back together again. We can now draw out some of the dimensions of this dialectical understanding of the church. On the basis of this tensive understanding of the church that exists in an interaction of two forces, one can derive some axioms for understanding the relationship between ecclesiology and congregational studies. The word "derived" is not used in the sense of an objective logical deduction. Rather, this co-construal of the elements constituting the church and regulating an approach to understanding suggests the three theses that follow.

2. *Congregational studies ultimately specifies the object studied by ecclesiology.* This statement is, in fact, contentious and would have to be argued ecclesiologically with churches that take the basic unit of the church to be the diocese or synod or some group larger than the congregation, but this argument can be made irenically.[9] On the supposition that the church experienced most directly and existentially is the congregation, however, the discipline whose focus is precisely that empirical historical community provides the first definition of the ecclesial community. Congregational studies analyzes on the ground the primary referent or subject matter of ecclesiology. The larger church consists in various forms of communion among these basic churches. This thesis therefore does not undermine the fact that many churches define their basic units on the larger scale of the diocese or synod.

3. *General ecclesiology, rather than field studies, determines the formal nature and mission of the church.* This thesis states that congregational studies does not define the formal nature and mission of the church, because that nature and mission is constituted by God, confessed in faith, and analyzed by theology as it manifests itself in all the churches. The specific difference or formal determining element that makes this religious community a Christian church lies in its confession of faith in the role of God in its life and the activities that relate it to God in response to God's initiative in its life. Roughly speaking, using a framework of hylomorphism, congregational studies describes the material object, while theology or ecclesiology specifies the formal dimension of the church. What makes the church truly church consists in God's power within it as chan-

---

9. One can distinguish between a basic unit of the church measured in terms of its existential influence on members (the congregation) from a basic unit measured in juridical terms (the diocese or synod). Because they are measured differently, what is said here relative to the congregation need not conflict with juridical boundaries.

neled to it through God's creative power revealed in Jesus Christ and experienced as God's Spirit. This does not mean that congregational studies lacks a formal theological component, for formal ecclesiology generally maintains that the whole church exists within the congregation.[10] Instead, the discipline of general or formal ecclesiology has a better purchase on the normative character of theology through its consultation with the many churches that include the congregations.

4. Congregational studies determines the credibility of the formal theological account of the church. This thesis states that congregational studies determines the credibility of a theological account of the church precisely by its concrete appeal to history, that is, by providing realism. Theology always tends toward the normative. Theology is not an exclusively empirical discipline, for it describes the way the church should be on the basis of the object of the community's faith in God as God is revealed in Jesus Christ. Theology's language frequently prescribes ideals and thus often seems at odds with what appears on the ground.[11] All are familiar with this language about the church. Congregational studies, which is the most specific and concrete historical approach to the church that is possible, is the anti-

---

10. Hans Küng writes eloquently of how the whole church is found in its many distinct manifestations: "There is, then, a multiplicity of local Churches (those of Ephesus, Philippi, Thessalonica, etc.) in which the one Church manifests itself: the Churches of individual towns and villages. And there is a multiplicity of regional Churches (the Church in Judea, Galilee, and Samaria, in Galatia, Macedonia, Asia, etc.) in which the one Church is also present: the Churches of individual provinces, dioceses, nations and continents. And finally there is a multiplicity of different types of Churches (the Hellenistic, the Judaeo-Christian, etc.) which often coincide with regional Churches but sometimes also, as a result of population movements, are dispersed throughout different regions: the Churches of different rites or denominations" (Hans Küng, *The Church* [New York: Sheed & Ward, 1967], p. 274). Note too the "essence" of the church that Paul says binds all the churches together because they all share in it: "There is one body and one Spirit, just as you were called to the one hope that belongs to your call, one Lord, one faith, one baptism, one God and Father of us all, who is above all and through all and in all" (Eph. 4:4-6). This essence is present in large communions and small particular congregations.

11. The marks of the church, which will be taken up in this chapter, provide an area where the connection between the language of the church about itself and what people observe is not obvious. Take the example of the church's holiness. It is important to recognize the objective dimension of the holiness of church institutions such as Scripture, sacrament, and the responsibility of office. But the simple assertion that the church is holy despite the sinfulness of its members seems paradoxical. The embarrassment felt by Catholics in North America in the wake of the revelation of clergy sexual abuse and cover-up indicates that the language of a "sinless church" lacks credibility in contemporary society.

dote to theological reductionism. Through congregational studies one can critically measure the credibility and ultimately the authenticity of the theological language about the church.

Illustration from the Marks of the Church

We now bring the theses argued in the previous section to bear upon an exemplary case. The case is drawn from an article by James Nieman that applies congregational studies as a way of lifting up a kind of lived theology that is implicitly forged by a congregation.[12] The focus on the marks of the church is suggested by the fact that this article clearly describes the nature and function of the marks of the church, and a comprehensive ecclesiology can scarcely omit commentary on this classical locus in the discipline. From the perspective of our part 1, the case readily illustrates the theses about the mutual influence of congregational studies and formal ecclesiology. This analysis of the marks will show, first, an example of how the marks are presented in congregational studies; second, how they are named and explained in theology; third and most important, how the empirical congregational perspective influences the theological claims.

1. By definition, congregational studies focuses on specific individual communities. It aims at understanding the particular community being studied and, by analogy, other communities like it. It is less a normative discipline, in the sense of applying external criteria, and more a search for the integrity of the inner logics of the congregation itself. Thus, from the perspective of congregational studies, Nieman presents the marks of the church as ideals or norms generated by the community out of their faith life that serve as criteria for self-evaluation. Traditionally, four such marks have been announced in the Nicene Creed as unity, catholicity, apostolicity, and holiness. These have also been multiplied by various theologians and churches to further specify ecclesial ideals. These qualities emerge from within the life of the community. They are not drawn from outside the community and do not measure other communities by comparison. All of them are "connected to the church's core experience of Christ as the one in and through whom we participate in the *missio Dei.*"[13] The marks

---

12. James Nieman, "Attending Locally: Theologies in Congregations," *International Journal of Practical Theology* 6 (2002): 198-225.

13. Nieman, "Attending Locally," p. 223.

of the church are "a way of naming the functions endemic to every local assembly in its own self-professed desire to be church, a standard that can only be assessed from within."[14] Nieman himself enumerates seven such marks of the church. These could be roughly correlated with the traditional four, but that is not the point for congregational studies. Rather he represents them as active qualities of a particular community that define it from within, and specify it by characterizing the life of its members in Christ and with one another in community. The marks define this community: "marks by which the wholeness and integrity of a congregation may be widely recognized (and therefore held *in common*) yet at the same time enacted in the ordinary ways endemic to a particular assembly (and therefore *commonplace*)."[15]

2. In contrast to congregational studies, the purview of general ecclesiology ranges over the entire history of the church. Even ecclesiology pursued from below is a far more abstract discipline than congregational studies. A theological account has to attend to the marks of the church provided by the historical tradition. Because of the scope of ecclesiology from below, attention must transcend the internal norms set by any particular community and look for those shared by all communities. Theology does not and cannot abandon its role as a normative discipline: its normativity is precisely what distinguishes it from an empirical social science such as history, sociology, or cultural anthropology. Theology searches for the norms that arise from the church's being related to God. It inevitably appeals to the New Testament. In effect, it looks for God's norms for the church at any given time. Surely these have to be interpreted anew in each new historical context in order to remain the "same." On the one hand, these norms are hardly external but arise from every congregation's life in Christ. On the other hand, because of the real internal relationship of all congregations to one another, these norms can appear to come from outside any given congregation, especially insofar as these norms are related to God's initiative that transcends all churches and is addressed to the churches from beyond themselves.

This transcendence deserves more comment. The theological tradition of the church speaks of four marks of the church: one, holy, catholic, and apostolic. In fact, the history of ecclesiology yields great variety in how these marks are interpreted. Of the many common features of the inter-

14. Nieman, "Attending Locally," p. 223.
15. Nieman, "Attending Locally," p. 224.

pretations, though, one stands out: the source of these marks or qualities is God, or God's grace, or the effectiveness of God's power in the community, what Schleiermacher (unfortunately) called the "invisible church." When the church truly exhibits these marks of authenticity, the community itself recognizes the power of God as the agent.

3. The fourth thesis in the second section above posited a dialectical interplay whereby congregational studies determines the credibility and the authenticity of theological claims. How does that work in the case of the marks of the church? In fact, the church does not appear to be one, holy, catholic, and apostolic, but precisely divided, resistant to communion, too fragmented for all the churches to be faithful to apostolic origins, and radically plagued by sin. If the marks of the church are not a theological sleight of hand, they must be brought down to earth and made to reflect the actual life of the congregations. Congregational studies thus serves as a kind of reality principle for formal ecclesiology, a test for whether the theological claims are credible.

One way to ensure this credibility would be to correlate the marks of the church in the sense discovered by congregational studies with those of formal theology. Nieman mentions seven marks and expresses them in terms of action: an integral church remembers its origins, confesses Christ, hopes or anticipates God's future, gathers and bonds as a community in response to God, orders its community life, engages the world in service of the values of the reign of God, and enters into some form of communion with other churches. It would not be difficult to find a rough parity between the traditional marks of the church and these actuated community ideals.

Another way to ensure credible formulations of the marks would be to explain the traditional marks of the church themselves in the realistic ways that congregational studies allows. In other words, allow the possibilities of actual communities to function as the measure for a realistic interpretation of the marks of the church. This exercise would show that unity can only be realistically predicated of a church that allows pluralism, that is, a unity that allows differences. Unity cannot mean uniformity. Catholicity will have to mean a universal wholeness and integrity of the great church in a communion among churches that acknowledge and accept real but valid differences among themselves. Churches cannot themselves be truly catholic without being open to other churches that are really different. Apostolicity will also have to recognize the pluralistic character of the church in the New Testament and the variety of different agencies that emerged in the earliest church for ensuring fidelity to tradition.[16] Finally, holiness will have to be understood as being based on God's grace which is at work within a congregation but in tension with the resistance to it that is called sin.

We conclude this first probe with a formula that expresses the relationship between general or formal ecclesiology (in this case, ecclesiology from below) and congregational studies. The two distinctive disciplines imply each other and interact dialectically, dynamically, and constructively. In an ecclesiology from below, congregational studies first directly examines from a primarily but not exclusively empirical perspective the object of ecclesiology, defining it concretely in its most elementary unit, the gathered community. Next, theology identifies the church as church through reflection on the symbols that convey God's relation to this community and the community's relation to God. Theology defines the church as a specifically religious and Christian organization. Finally, congregational studies chastens the normative claims of theology with real possibility, making them credible. In the end, this formula envisages a friendly and fruitful relationship between these two disciplines.

Part 2: From the Perspective of Congregational Studies

Part 1 of this chapter has upheld the ecclesiological side of our joint discussion. Part 2 will address the same relationship from the perspective of congregational studies. It too is divided into three subsections. The first will define the perspective assumed by congregational studies as it is represented here. The second will lay out four theses that draw out that perspective in more detail. The final section will reflect on the new challenges and possibilities opened up by a partnership between formal ecclesiology and congregational studies.

---

16. The historical vehicles for ensuring fidelity to origins and unity among the churches in the earliest church were many: recourse to the Jewish Scriptures, the formation of a New Testament canon, agreement on central festal dates and liturgical formulas, solidification of the structure of leadership in the monarchical episcopate (where bishops were analogous to a pastor in the later church), succession in ministry to mirror continuity of community Christian life, manuals of discipline, interchurch meetings, visitations, and leaders of neighboring churches laying hands on new bishops of other churches, among other interchanges.

A Perspective on Congregational Studies

The view of congregational studies adopted here should not be confused with a kind of ethnography without remainder. Instead, our perspective is rooted in the field of practical theology, including its special focus on studying congregations and the local theologies expressed therein. Practical theology implies that theology, as the church's distinctive discourse, provides the appropriate way to open up the special ecclesial character of particular Christian assemblies. In other words, when we begin to sense the theological work of congregations, then we are seeing the church acting as church rather than as some other similarly sized and structured nonprofit organizations. Our interest in studying congregations, therefore, lies in the hope that, when they recognize through this theological work their own distinctive character as church, they can better assess their own identity, mission, and health.

This means that congregational studies, as understood here, presumes an intersection between social research methods and the field of theology, a point that will be developed and refined in what follows. On the one hand, this approach relies on ethnographic tools, but only insofar as they are useful for disclosing local theologies. There are certainly many other valid and useful ways to use ethnography to study congregations (as organizations, subcultures, and so forth), but the point here is to focus social research on what is distinctive about these groups as church. On the other hand, the method advocated here relies on the field of theology, but with greater weight on primary theology found in congregational action (what Aidan Kavanagh once called "the church caught in the act of being most overtly itself"[17]) than on the secondary reflections and systems typical in the academy.[18] This statement intends neither to restrict theology to church life nor to denigrate the value of academic theological insight, but instead to ensure an attitude attuned to the ecclesial purposes of theology enacted by its basic users — a commitment that does challenge some scholars to revise their perceptions of what counts as theology. In sum, congregational studies should treat theology as its proper aim and focus, for the sake of enabling congregations to claim an ample, distinctive role as

---

17. Aidan Kavanagh, *On Liturgical Theology: The Hale Memorial Lectures of Seabury-Western Theological Seminary, 1981* (New York: Pueblo, 1984), p. 75.

18. Edward Farley, "Interpreting Situations: An Inquiry into the Nature of Practical Theology," in *Formation and Reflection: The Promise of Practical Theology,* ed. Lewis S. Mudge and James N. Poling (Philadelphia: Fortress, 1987), p. 9.

church in the world. Part 1 of this chapter argued from formal ecclesiology to the need of concrete empirical studies. The goal of part 2 is now to propose, from the perspective of congregational studies, how the field of theology might be a helpful partner in this process. We will pursue this goal in four interrelated theses.

Before turning to them, however, it is important to note how we refer to the respective fields of congregational studies (using ethnographic and other tools) and theology (especially that part concerned with ecclesiology). As a matter of convenience, we have spoken of each in a rather unitary fashion as separate, internally cohesive areas of study. This is only a convenience, however, for things are not quite so neat. As the few published histories of congregational studies[19] and the vast range of current research about congregations make quite clear, "congregational studies" is an umbrella term, so that what more-or-less coheres as the field referenced by that term cannot be considered just one thing. This is partly due to the diversity of methods employed, with some approaches relying on qualitative and ethnographic tools, others on quantitative forms and comparisons, and still others on mixed strategies. In addition, the plurality of methods in congregational studies is due to varied aims of research, such as whether the study relates congregations to comparable social and cultural phenomena, or whether it is engaged with the church and its theological commitments.[20]

By the same token, of course, the field of theology is also no unified reality. Historical, systematic, or philosophical theologians, for example,

---

19. See James F. Hopewell, *Congregation: Stories and Structures*, ed. Barbara G. Wheeler (Philadelphia: Fortress, 1987), pp. 19-39; and Allison Stokes and David A. Roozen, "The Unfolding Study of Congregational Studies," in *Carriers of Faith-Lessons from Congregational Studies*, ed. Carl S. Dudley, Jackson W. Carroll, and James P. Wind (Louisville: Westminster John Knox, 1991), pp. 183-92.

20. The point is not to criticize or invalidate other approaches but to be clear that there are distinctive commitments in various forms of congregational studies. For example, some who study congregations focus on the cultural dimensions a local church manifested in its symbolic work or group processes. Their approach leans on tools drawn from ethnography, the embedded fieldwork central to cultural anthropology that is used for observing and describing human activity. (See, for example, Nancy Ammerman, *Bible Believers: Fundamentalists in the Modern World* [New Brunswick, NJ: Rutgers University Press, 1987].) By contrast, others are more interested in exploring demographic contours across many congregations. Their approach uses quite different methods, such as survey instruments and statistical analysis, that are characteristic of quantitative sociology. (See, for example, Mark Chaves, *Congregations in America* [Cambridge, MA: Harvard University Press, 2004].)

are naturally more interested in textual sources or in the interrelation of ideas. Given this important role in the larger ecology of theological studies, these theologians may rightly have little direct interest in the concrete situations of and activities in living congregations. Even when we consider only the theological subfield of ecclesiology, various branches focus their attention on broader questions such as ecumenism, matters of organization and polity, or links to other doctrines. An ecclesiology from below, sympathetic as it is to partnership with congregational studies, is but one part of this complicated disciplinary picture.[21]

Four Theses on the Relation of Congregational Studies and General Ecclesiology

With these cautions in mind, we turn now to four theses that express, from the perspective of congregational studies elaborated above, how that field relates to general ecclesiology. As with those offered in part 1 of this chapter, the theses below begin with a foundational claim about the relationship between the empirical/historical and the theological. The three remaining theses unfold the implications of the first: on the question of how the study of congregations should therefore be focused, on the dual moves such study should incorporate, and on the reflectively critical aims that study should seek.

1. *The study of congregations needs more than ethnographic tools.* Since theology is not simply a game of ideas in the rarified atmosphere of the academy, we find it tangibly unfolding in other arenas as well, including congregational life. While it is more obvious in ritual actions and more subtle and fragmented in meetings, work projects, conversations, or budgets, theological work potentially happens throughout a congregation. We say "potentially" because, of course, sometimes a budget is just a budget. What makes ethnographic tools so valuable in this regard is that they provide a discipline for closely and deeply attending to the empirical forms theology can take. In field research, the qualitative methods of par-

---

21. Again, the point is not a complaint about other ways of doing theology. In fact, what follows will show that we need them, even if they have little initial interest in congregations. This means, however, that we must first discover those persons in ecclesiology and theology who are willing to be partners and enter into a basic conversation about congregations as such, and then call upon these partners to interpret what we are doing within their larger disciplines.

ticipant observation, semistructured interviews, artifact and place study, and document analysis are used to attend to what is happening theologically. Such tools not only help us notice theological work but also connect this work to other human and material matters in the congregation, so that theology is not left insulated from social and cultural realities but fully implicated in them. Moreover, as we noted in part 1, empirical research provides a credibility test for theological reflection about the church, helping even ecclesiology done from below to be more grounded and realistic.

Ethnographic tools cannot do this alone, however; the field of theology is needed in two closely related ways. First, out of the many things to notice in a congregation, how do we know what counts as theological activity? To use an earlier example, ethnography is poorly equipped to distinguish when a budget makes a theological claim or when it is simply a budget. Congregational studies, therefore, looks to the field of theology to attend not only to its customary focus on doctrines and texts but also to the less familiar but equally complicated matter of the ordinary, concrete ways people do theology through their actions, resources, gatherings, and so forth. Second, once we are clearer about what counts as theology, do ethnographic methods still sometimes get in the way? If research tools assume that religious activity is driven only by secular motivations, for example, it is doubtful one can take theological realities very seriously.[22] While it is typically the case that ethnography is far less biased than this, perhaps other tools would be even more attuned to the "theological frequency" of congregational life. In a different project, Nieman has begun to explore whether methods originating in narratology, cognitive task analysis, social semiotics, esthetic appreciation, and normative case studies might be more sensitive to theology as it happens in local assemblies.[23] Here again, however, these tools often arise from nontheological fields. Therefore, the field of theology can help us discern whether these or other

22. The pervasive tendency of some forms of social research to reduce all human behavior to "rational choice" explanations (i.e., that people are little more than cost-benefit calculators) is but one instance of how methodological commitments may obstruct the ability to see other motivations (such as religious or theological ones) active within groups. For an extended critique of rational choice explanations, see Christian Smith, *Moral, Believing Animals: Human Personhood and Culture* (New York: Oxford University Press, 2003).

23. This research is supported by the Lilly Endowment, Inc., through a grant titled "Discerning Theologies: New Methods for Studying Congregations," grant #2006-0027-00.

new tools inadvertently import unhelpful biases that impede our ability to see theology at work locally.

✓2. *The study of congregations should focus on practices.* This thesis may sound at odds with the second thesis of part 1, that the congregation ought to be specified as our object of study. There we argued that the empirical, historical community is the form of church that people experience most directly, which is what congregational studies analyzes and what ecclesiology should treat as its primary referent (rather than larger forms of association among these basic communities). This impulse can be extended further, however. Those who study congregations know how difficult it can be to specify where the boundaries of such groups are actually located. Religious behavior, identity formation, and so forth occur in diverse parts of the lives of congregants, even if they receive quite concentrated attention within the congregation. Our focus should therefore be on the activity of those who gather through congregations, theological work that may well extend beyond the congregation itself, rather than assuming that the arbitrary and often vague social boundaries of such a group will suffice to specify what we are studying. Toward this end, although we begin by looking at the empirical reality of the congregation as a group, our real focus should be on the practices enacted therein.

Confines of space prevent our elaborating the rich conversation emerging in many fields about what constitutes a practice. Elsewhere, Nieman has argued that any practice has five basic features: it involves tangible actions, is socially embedded, is meaningful for participants, offers strategies for right use, and seeks an intended purpose.[24] In relation to studying congregations, such a view of practices would give further focus to what we examine. Empirical research would look at these concrete, shared, meaningful activities, how they are done and for what reasons. Rather than saying that we study the congregation in general, we would look at these particulars, tease them apart, understand them more deeply, and connect similar practices in terms of how they work within and beyond the congregation's life.[25] This is fine as far as it goes, but just because

24. James Nieman, "The Idea of Practice and Why It Matters in the Teaching of Preaching," *Teaching Theology and Religion* 11 (2008): 123-33.

25. Such an approach can therefore be located within the stream that Nicholas Healy characterizes "by a concern to 'bring to discourse' or make explicit the often overlooked or taken-for-granted practices of the churches and congregations so that they may be brought into closer conformity with the word of God. Here attention is directed to the practices themselves, which are critically and constructively analyzed in light of contemporary chal-

a practice is important in a group does not necessarily mean it is theologically telling. Therefore, the real value of any practice is understood in terms of a field of interpretation by which it makes sense. (For example, the practice of pitching makes quite different sense if the field of interpretation is baseball, cricket, or horseshoes.) This is where theology can again enter in, to help frame the connections (if any) between a pattern of practices in a congregation and the larger interpretive field of theology. Looking at practices therefore affords a way not only to focus empirical research, but especially to link what we discover in congregations to the broader field of interpretation that is the ambit of formal theological reflection.

3. *The study of congregations is both descriptive and prescriptive.* In the brief history of congregational studies, a thesis like this amounts to stepping into a minefield. Some ardently defend that such research should be purely descriptive and hold no further stake in the matter. Again, we may rightly doubt whether this really happens so neatly. Frequently, simply conducting field research, let alone sharing that information with congregants, initiates a process of local reflection and assessment that soon becomes a catalyst for change. Descriptive work already carries the seeds for prescriptive work. Prescriptive tendencies still happen no matter whether we try to bracket them out or how subtly they emerge. Since the point in studying congregations, as advocated here, is to assist in their identity, mission, and health, this does not appear as a problem. Those who study congregations should simply acknowledge both of these dimensions, which have elsewhere been called the indicative and subjunctive sides of practical theology: the "what is" and "what might be" of the congregation.[26] Moreover, this acknowledgment can happen without necessarily leading to the heavy-handed imposition of advice, programs, or other consultant agendas, which is usually what we fear when treading onto prescriptive terrain.

Of course, it is one thing to say that we should also attend to the prescriptive side of studying congregations, quite another to say how this would work. How do we go a step further to pose challenges, raise alternatives, and contribute to a larger critical and strategic task without harming

---

lenges (theological and others) and, as it may be, abandoned, changed, reconstructed or maintained unaltered." Nicholas M. Healy, "Practices and the New Ecclesiology: Misplaced Concreteness?" *International Journal of Systematic Theology* 5 (2003): 290-91.

26. Kathleen A. Cahalan and James R. Nieman, "Mapping the Field of Practical Theology," in *For Life Abundant: Practical Theology, Theological Education, and Christian Ministry*, ed. Dorothy C. Bass and Craig Dykstra (Grand Rapids: Eerdmans, 2008), pp. 62-85.

those we study? Theology could play a key role in this further step by revisiting how the marks of the church help with assessing local theological practices. We need not return to the Reformation-era debates that used these marks in an exclusionary, competitive, and essentialist rhetoric to assert who was truly church and who was not. A more irenic approach might be mediated through the so-called Nicene marks of unity, holiness, catholicity, and apostolicity as noted in part 1.[27] Whether this list or another, such marks express the integrity of the *missio Dei* in which any form of the church participates. Too often, congregations are judged by externally imposed standards (size, diversity, programs), which leaves most people feeling inadequate on some scale or another. By assessing local practices in terms of historic marks, however, the standards become internal to the character of every church as body of Christ.[28] Theologians could therefore help congregations assess their particular ways of embodying this character, rather than leave them subject to depleting comparisons only with each other. This prescriptive dimension then becomes the natural counterpoint to the descriptive, a clear picture of local practices answered by an honest challenge about how these might be more faithfully enacted for the sake of a witness common to all assemblies.

4. *The study of congregations should reclaim theological reflection.* One complaint about congregational studies in some quarters is that it contributes to the objectification of local assemblies. Congregations become passive vessels studied by outside experts, which reinforces their already diminished sense of agency in a complex and demanding social ecology. Whether or not this objectification actually occurs, the complaint raises the legitimate concern that it may not be enough that such research amasses insights about congregations, but that it also should help them become more active agents in their public role as church. One place this

27. As to whether these four should actually be called "marks of the church," see Gordon W. Lathrop and Timothy J. Wengert, *Christian Assembly: Marks of the Church in a Pluralistic Age* (Minneapolis: Augsburg Fortress, 2004), pp. 17-18.

28. In this respect, the so-called Nicene marks are especially revealing. They occur in the context of a creed by which the believer professes a relationship with the triune God. That is, marks are not abstract organizational criteria or group standards, but are rooted in a living relationship with the God known chiefly through Christ Jesus and tangibly manifested by the Spirit's power through the concrete forms of the church. When congregations assess themselves, each in their own ways, in light of such marks, they are then asking how they make a particular witness to God's ways for us, and to human thriving in light of such divine initiative.

turn toward active agency is particularly poignant relates to theology. We earlier noted that congregations embody primary theological work. Even so, how often are those primary forms of theology subjected to a probing, informed review at the local level? Lacking this critical dimension, congregations become atrophied at theological reflection and risk remaining entrenched in what are literally parochial behaviors. There seems to be an ethical responsibility for those who study congregations to take up an educational aim in that work, drawing congregations into the secondary analysis of their primary theological practices for the sake of their long-term health and thriving.

One way this educational aim could happen is simply for theologians to generate the kind of historical and comparative ecclesiology from below that has been introduced by Haight.[29] Presented with accessible resources about the many concrete ways congregations have operated faithfully in other times and places, contemporary assemblies can thereby encounter new practices, move beyond how things have always been done, and draw their own prescriptive conclusions. Beyond this, we also need to reconnect particular assemblies with the larger stream of faithful practices to which all congregations are beholden in their catholicity (i.e., wholeness or integrity). Although the primary unit of the church that people experience is the congregation, the latest published round of the U.S. Lutheran–Roman Catholic dialogue reminds us that there is another way to speak of the local church: that of the regional network overseen by those called to that task (like a diocese or synod led by a bishop, but not strictly that historical arrangement).[30] The connection between mutually accountable assemblies is also an ancient, venerable way to think of the local church, with clear advantages in our highly eclectic and privatized society. How might theologians enrich the study of congregations by helping assemblies claim again the responsibility they have to one another in a particular locale? All this is to reassert an agenda of theological education, reconnecting specific congregations with the larger wisdom of the entire church, and for reasons far beyond mere compliance or cooperation.

29. Roger Haight, *Christian Community in History*, 3 vols. (New York: Continuum, 2004 8).

30. Randall Lee and Jeffrey Gros, eds., *The Church as Koinonia of Salvation: Its Structures and Ministries*, Common Statement of the Tenth Round of the U.S. Lutheran–Roman Catholic Dialogue, pref. Charles Maahs and Richard Sklba (Washington, DC: United States Conference of Catholic Bishops, 2004), nos. 41-46.

New Challenges and Possibilities for Ecclesiology

Although one might add or subtract from the four theses above, we now move on to complicate them further. In particular, we want to consider now the opportunities these proposals offer respectively to the field of theology and to the ethnographic study of congregations, and in so doing point to several unresolved challenges that remain on the table.

1. For the field of theology, we have noted that a closer connection with congregational studies would grant the opportunity for a reality check, particularly in the area of ecclesiology. If we are interested in theology that stands in service to the church, then it is essential that it engage accurately and amply with the local realities, sorrows, and hopes of actual assemblies of the faithful. Without this check, theological study can risk becoming insulated from the world in which it tries to speak, and thus its gifts of wisdom and reflection become muted or subverted. Not only is the field of theology hurt by this, but congregations also desperately need the connections, perspectives, and mediation theology can bring.[31]

This opportunity carries with it significant challenges at two different levels. First, at a basic level of operation, it assumes we really know what counts as a "credibility test" for theology. That is, simply because study of a congregation using ethnographic tools might reveal what actually is the case, in what respect would we say that information should or should not reshape what we think theologically? This question of what counts as evidence for validity or credibility remains a contested issue in the use of qualitative ethnographic tools alone,[32] and only becomes more complex when we try to turn the criteria that govern one field of inquiry to

31. As Schillebeeckx once remarked, "the subject of the interpretation of faith is not really the theologian but the Christian communities of faith themselves — the church in its broad spectrum and its cultural distribution over many centres. Here theology is merely a help to the community of faith. Academic theology then tries to integrate the new experiences, the new praxis and the reflections of local communities into the totality of the 'church's recollection' and into the great reserves of the experiences of faith of the whole church down the ages. Theology thus at the same time prevents these new experiences from remaining sporadic or ultimately causing disintegration. Thus academic theology 'mediates' to the base the rich experiential traditions in the churches down the ages, and prevents the base from being cognitively isolated. Theology itself is enriched by the new experiences and reflections from theology which grows in and from the life of the communities of faith" (Schillebeeckx, *Church*, p. 35).

32. See John Swinton and Harriet Mowat, *Practical Theology and Qualitative Research* (London: SCM, 2006), pp. 121-24.

serve as tests in quite another field. We need to give greater thought to how the empirical features of congregations can actually serve as a reality check for theologians attentive to local assemblies.

Second, at a deeper level of engagement, the effort to use descriptive material as part of an integrated and responsible theological reflection raises the perennial issue of the place for human experience or the empirical situation in the field of theology. The proposition of part 1, that congregational studies describes the material object of the church while theology or ecclesiology specifies its formal dimension, leaves open the thorny issue of how the concrete and the spiritual dimensions of the church relate. Although it cannot be elaborated here, Schillebeeckx's discussion of the relation between experience and revelation offers a useful starting point for a conversation on this issue.[33] There are doubtless other ways to begin as well. In the end, we need to face this deeper issue if we wish to relate ethnography and ecclesiology over the long run, especially to avoid the presumption that either field can determine in isolation from the other whether or how empirical realities make a difference.

2. Turning to the ethnographic study of congregations, the broad claim in this part of the discussion has been that a closer relationship with theology brings the opportunity for attending more closely to the distinctive character of the church. The underlying concern here is to preclude any tendency toward a sociological or historicist reduction of the church only to its human scale. More than this, however, the aim is to appreciate more completely what faithful people claim to be doing when they gather as church. If we are not simply imposing a "bad faith" assumption on this claim from the outset, then congregational studies should look at the entire range of what local assemblies practice and hope, which includes the theological.

This opportunity of naming the identity of the church is linked to two further implications that may be considered unresolved challenges. The first involves the thesis that congregational studies, although clearly a descriptive enterprise, is also unavoidably normative and should therefore accept that role and engage it intentionally. In truth, we did not go very far to say how this should happen or what its limits might be. A few years ago, Nieman worked to assemble the history of the Congregational Studies Project Team, a small group that has, for nearly thirty years, produced and refined some of the most important teaching resources in the field. In the

---

33. See Schillebeeckx, *Church*, pp. 15-28.

course of reviewing their archives and interviewing every living person on that team, it quickly became apparent how early this issue of normativity began to dog their work and was built into the fabric of the field. How do we steer a course between the Scylla of uninvested description and the Charybdis of disempowering consultancy? This is a question that will not disappear, and if we want congregational studies to be engaged with both the "is" and the "might be" of the church, it requires our sustained attention now.

A second implication that appears challenging concerns the scope of what we study when we look at congregations. Here again, theology is shifting our attention in both narrower and broader directions. In the narrower direction, the study of congregations needs to develop a robust dialogue with practical theology in order to understand more closely how to analyze a practice as theological work. This will be crucial if we expect to be more precise in our work, and avoid general overviews of congregations that can bury us in data and numb the power of insight. In the broader direction, the study of congregations needs to explore how the historical and ecumenical insight about the local church as a network might expand the field's view of congregations. To be sure, several excellent sociological studies have adopted this scale of attention,[34] but the challenge is to make this part of the ordinary approach of congregational studies, resulting not only from reasons of sound social but also of good theological research.

We conclude this second probe by stressing that, aside from the opportunities and challenges in both fields, the main reason congregational studies needs theology, and vice versa, concerns the benefit for actual congregations. The great strength of ethnographic methods is that they offer the tools for disciplined self-awareness, a critical consciousness for congregations in a descriptive vein. Enhancing this descriptive power, the great strength of theological studies is that it offers a way to reconnect with a wider tradition and discover genuine alternatives for action, a critical consciousness for congregations in a prescriptive vein. Both fields help congregations recognize their roots in a wider wisdom and their accountabil-

---

34. See Nancy Ammerman, *Pillars of Faith: American Congregations and Their Partners* (Berkeley: University of California Press, 2005); Penny Edgell Becker, *Congregations in Conflict: Cultural Models of Local Religious Life* (New York: Cambridge University Press, 1999); Nancy L. Eiesland, *A Particular Place: Urban Restructuring and Religious Ecology in a Southern Exurb* (Piscataway, NJ: Rutgers University Press, 2000); and Omar M. McRoberts, *Streets of Glory: Church and Community in a Black Urban Neighborhood* (Chicago: University of Chicago Press, 2003).

ity to other partners, and thus leave congregations more attuned to being the church than when left to themselves. If this is the end we keep before us in our ethnographic and ecclesiological interest in congregations, not only will our respective fields be enriched, but the faithful communities they study as well.

Conclusion

In the end, this chapter is located in a longstanding scholarly conversation about how to understand the church both faithfully and realistically. Our remarks offer two contemporary, discipline-based responses to a cluster of questions raised by James Gustafson nearly half a century ago:

> How can the same phenomenon, the Church, be understood from two radically diverse perspectives? Does the use of doctrinal language require inherently the language of social thought? Does a social interpretation of the Church necessarily exclude the more distinctively theological and doctrinal interpretation? If the two are not mutually exclusive, how can the significance of the social processes and elements be theologically understood?[35]

As they are each portrayed in this chapter, ecclesiology and congregational studies offer complementary ways for holding together social and theological understandings of the church in its local reality. Their mutual relevance for one another is not just a happy coincidence of recent trends but suggests a more holistic interest in understanding the church. We no longer ought to be satisfied with approaches that reduce ecclesial existence to its functions and processes on the one hand or its ideas and ideals on the other. The alternative offered by the two fields discussed above holds the social and theological aspects of church in healthy tension. This alternative promises not only scholarship that renders a more accurate sense of what the church truly is today, but also a more holistic vision for what it can yet become as a sign of Christ's life for the world.

---

35. Gustafson, *Treasure in Earthen Vessels*, p. 100.

CHAPTER 2

Ecclesiology and Empirical Research on the Church

Harald Hegstad

A New Situation in Theological Research — and Some Unsolved Questions

The last years we have experienced a growing interest in empirical research on churches and congregations. This is for instance expressed in the fact that "congregational studies" has been established as a field of research. An important aspect in these studies has been the employment of ethnographic methods in the study of local congregations, using fieldwork, participatory observation, and depth interviews. A characteristic of this growing research is its interdisciplinarity, not only based in the social sciences in a narrow sense. What is especially noteworthy is the extent this type of research has been taken up by theologians and in theological institutions. Theologians are cooperating with social scientists in the field, and they are themselves engaging in empirical research.

This development is remarkable given a tradition of general distrust in theology regarding the source value of human experience. This distrust was especially prominent in traditions like the Barthian, which understood its role primarily as an interpreter of divine revelation. In this line of thinking the empirical field is reduced to a field of *application* of theological insights gained from the theological work. Knowledge of the empirical field has primarily a practical value, securing the efficiency of the dissemination of nonempirical theological insights.

Coming from a Norwegian, Lutheran tradition, I am rather familiar with this way of thinking. In my dissertation I analyzed the understanding of experience and revelation in the theology of the Norwegian theologian Leiv Aalen.[1] In his understanding of these questions, Aalen was basically influenced by the dialectical theology of the 1930s (especially that of Karl Barth and Emil Brunner). His strategy, as I interpreted it, was to isolate revelation from human experience, limiting it to the cognitive content of the Bible, as the object of faith. In his opinion, it is not possible to have a direct experience of God and divine reality. In my dissertation, I criticized this understanding as problematic in relation to the theology of incarnation: doesn't God becoming human really mean that he makes himself an object for human experience?

Similar types of critique are rather commonplace these days. Experience is definitely back in the general theological discourse. However, when doing empirical research, reference to experience in a general sense is not sufficient. This type of research is working with the concept of *empirical data*, that is, data from the world of experience collected in a methodologically qualified way. Empirical data are what can be observed and registered. In this context only scientific theories based on empirical data may be regarded as valid theories. A general and unspecified reference to experience is not sufficient.

Including empirical perspectives puts new demands on theology in several ways. On the one hand it raises the question of how this type of research should be included in theology. For good reasons a purely interdisciplinary approach is insufficient. Theologians should not limit themselves to learning from and working together with social scientists and others; they should also include empirical research in their own disciplinary work. The need for an "empirical theology" has forcefully been argued by the Dutch theologian Johannes A. van der Ven.[2] According to this program, theology should include empirical methods in its repertoire of methods or perspectives, as it has already included those from other fields (e.g., historical science and philosophy). Theology itself should become empirical. A theologian working in this field should himself master empirical methods and social-scientific perspectives! This does not exclude the necessity for interdisciplinary collaboration with social scientists who are not themselves theologians: theology should make use of insights and results from

---

1. Harald Hegstad, *Transcendens og inkarnasjon. Troserkjennelsens problem i Leiv Aalens teologi* (Oslo: Solum, 1993).

2. Johannes A. van der Ven, *Practical Theology: An Empirical Approach* (Kampen: Kok Pharos, 1993).

the general social sciences, and follow the same methodological standards in its own work. Using this strategy for isolating theology as a separated "Christian sociology" etc. is a dangerous strategy.

Including empirical perspectives in theology does not only raise methodological considerations, but also fundamental issues related to the understanding of theology, its object and its content. What is the object of theology, and is this object within the world of experience? This type of question becomes most acute when it comes to ecclesiology, that is, the theological understanding of the church. A basic question is the understanding of the relation between the church as an object of faith and as experienced reality. What is the relation between the "one, holy, catholic, and apostolic church" that is confessed in the Nicene Creed and the complex social reality we also call church? Do theological ecclesiology and the empirical study of the church have the same object?

In Protestant theology, there has been a tradition of distinguishing between the "visible church" on the one hand and the "invisible" or "hidden church" on the other. This tradition is an important background for understanding the problems of relating theological ecclesiology and empirical investigation of the church to each other. The question is: In what way is ecclesiology able to relate to the empirical church in all its complexity? Are we really talking about an ecclesiology of the empirical church?

On the one hand this is a challenge to theological ecclesiology, which traditionally has been working with the idea of the church rather than the church as it is historically and empirically given. Is its understanding of its object sufficient when it is only loosely connected to experienced reality? On the other hand this is a challenge to empirical research on churches and congregations in a theological context: What is the object of this research in theological terms? Does empirical research on churches and congregations deal with the church in its theological meaning, or only with its outer appearance? And in what way may insights from such empirical investigation have relevance for theological reflection?

Bonhoeffer's Dogmatic Inquiry into the Sociology of the Church

To a great extent, these questions have been neglected by theology until recently. An early exception was the young Dietrich Bonhoeffer. In his 1927 dissertation *Sanctorum Communio* he raises this question. The subtitle states the main perspective of the work: *A Dogmatic Inquiry into the Sociol-*

ogy of the Church. The aim of the book is not the writing of a sociology of religion or an investigation into the relation between sociology and theology in general. Bonhoeffer's study is a *dogmatic* inquiry on the church, and he is interested in the theological understanding of the church. This means, however, the church as a real community, not as a pure idea. On the one hand he points to the fact that the church is more than what is empirically evident, a fact that corresponds to basic differences in the sociological and the theological perspectives on the church, but his basic concern is to keep the two perspectives together, and he insists that theological statements on the church refer to the same church to which sociological statements refer. The traditional dichotomy between visible and invisible churches is most unsatisfactory, in his opinion.

> We do not believe in an invisible church, nor in the kingdom of God existing in the church as *coetus electorum;* but we believe that God has made the actual empirical church, in which the Word and the sacraments are administered, into his community, that is the Body of Christ. . . . We believe in the church not as an unattainable ideal, or one which has still to be attained, but as a present reality.[3]

In retrospect, Bonhoeffer's way of posing the question was more important than his attempt to answer it. This is to a great extent because Bonhoeffer takes his concept of sociology and social reality from a rather idealistic and speculative form of sociology (the so-called formalistic school), which was quite dominant in Germany at the time. In consequence there is no real interest in utilizing empirical data in the understanding of the church — the sociology of the church is in a way decided by the act of defining it.[4]

Healy's Critique of Abstract Ecclesiologies and His Practical-Prophetic Alternative

A much more recent contribution is presented by Nicholas M. Healy in his book *Church, World and the Christian Life* (2000). Healy's book is a funda-

---

3. Dietrich Bonhoeffer, *Sanctorum Communio: A Dogmatic Inquiry into the Sociology of the Church* (London: Collins, 1963), p. 197. Cf. Harald Hegstad, "Sanctorum Communio. Dietrich Bonhoeffers forståelse av forholdet mellom ekklesiologi og sosiologi," in *Forskning og fundering,* ed. Erling Birkedal et al. (Trondheim: Tapir, 2000), pp. 251-64.

4. Cf. the convincing critique in Peter Berger, "Sociology and Ecclesiology," in *The Place of Bonhoeffer,* ed. Martin Marty (London: SCM, 1963), pp. 53-79.

mental critique of the general tendency in modern ecclesiology of working with concepts and models of the church, rather than the concrete church as it is. In his own words:

> In general ecclesiology in our period has become highly systematic and theoretical, focused more upon discerning the right things to think about the church rather than oriented to the living, rather messy, confused and confusing body that the church actually is.[5]

One characteristic of this type of ecclesiology is that it is *abstract:* It is oriented toward the theoretical *essence* of the church, rather than its actual existence. On the other hand this leads to an idealized understanding of the church: The church is seen in its *perfection,* rather than in its real condition. This leads to an understanding, either explicit or as an implicit consequence, of the church as free of sin. As far as it is recognized, it is seen "merely as an empirical distortion of the church's true theological identity."[6] The obvious danger of this way of thinking is ecclesial pride.

According to Healy this way of thinking represents a type of theological reductionism, which is no better than the opposing sociological reductionism that reduces the church to a purely human community. As a fully human community that is imperfect and sinful, the church at the same time is God's church.

Healy challenges ecclesiology on two fundamental questions. One is related to the *methodological* question: How should we do ecclesiology? His answer is that ecclesiology should be a discipline that is working with the empirical church, the church as it is. This does not mean that it loses its theological, normative perspective and foundation. He is rather critical of correlational models of the relation between theology and social sciences (e.g., Don Browning and the above-mentioned J. van der Ven).[7] Even when we are working with the empirical church, the discourse should be fundamentally theological.

Doing ecclesiology with the concrete church also means that ecclesiology is not oriented toward essence, but toward practice. The task of ecclesiology is to aid the church in its basic tasks, according to Healy "to witness to its Lord in the world and to help the individual Christian in her

---

5. Nicholas M. Healy, *Church, World, and the Christian Life: Practical-Prophetic Ecclesiology* (Cambridge: Cambridge University Press, 2000), p. 3.

6. Healy, *Church,* p. 10.

7. Healy, *Church,* p. 49.

task of discipleship."[8] Healy finds the theological horizon for this in the "theodramatic theory" of Hans Urs von Balthasar. Ecclesiology should thus be developed into a "practical-prophetic ecclesiology" that "focuses theological attention upon the church's confused and sometimes sinful daily life."[9] In order to achieve this, Healy argues for the use of disciplines like history, sociology, and ethnography. He does not want, however, to use these disciplines as they are — referring to John Milbank, he argues for "a theological form of sociology" or a "Christian sociology" or an "ecclesiological ethnography."[10] How this type of Christian sociology or ethnography is to be done is rather unclear, and I am not convinced that this way of isolating a theological use of sociology from sociology in general takes into account the fact that the church as an empirical reality is a part of the world and should be investigated with methods used for investigating the world in general. On the other hand I do agree that sociological methods and perspectives have to be integrated and made fruitful within the theological interpretation of the church. There are still issues to be clarified on this methodological level in the process toward an ecclesiology that deals with the empirical church.

The other challenge from Healy, in my opinion, lies in the question about the *ontology of the church*. What is the core identity of the church, and what distinguishes it from other social or religious groups? Healy's position is not to look for a hidden essence behind the concrete church, but to understand *the concrete church as the church* in every sense of the word. What qualifies the church as church in a theological sense is the understanding of the church as part of God's story. The church is on its way, *in via*, toward eschatological fulfillment. What makes the church different are not its inherent qualities, but its relation or orientation toward the triune God: "I suggest that what renders the church unique and superior to all other religious and non-religious bodies is . . . its Spirit-empowered *orientation* to Jesus Christ and through him, to the triune God."[11] The identity of the church is not in its hidden and true essence, but in its relation to an eschatological future and to the God who is leading history toward its end.

Healy's understanding of the church is very much oriented toward the practices of the church. How should the church act in the world in or-

---

8. Healy, *Church,* p. 74.
9. Healy, *Church,* pp. 154-55.
10. Healy, *Church,* pp. 166-69.
11. Healy, *Church,* p. 17.

der to solve its tasks? One question arises from this question: How then is *God* acting with the church; where do we find *God's* acts in the world? Healy answers this question with the only possible answer, that God is acting through human acts: "Both divine and human agency . . . must be understood . . . without any kind of division of labor."[12] At the same time, it is necessary to add: since human action is also an expression of *sin,* the acts of God have to be detected in the light of the revelation in Scripture.

A Social Practice That Constitutes the Church?

Healy does not, however, answer the question whether there are certain human practices above others in which God communicates himself to humans and thereby constitutes the church. As a Lutheran I simply miss a sort of sacramental center in the theology of this Catholic theologian! Among all the practices the church may engage in, one is fundamental to its very existence. That is to come together in the name of Jesus, to seek God in the Spirit, through the gospel, through the sharing of bread and wine.

In company with Miroslav Volf and others I understand the identity of the church in the light of Matthew 18:20: "For where two or three are gathered in my name, I am there among them."[13] As Volf points out, this promise connects the church to the eschatological assembly, the community of mankind with God in the kingdom, an anticipation of something not yet fulfilled. What constitutes this anticipation is the relation of this community to the risen Christ: From this perspective the existence of the church as something more than a religious community is a fulfillment of Christ's promise that can only be encountered in faith.[14]

Such an understanding of the church presupposes viewing the church in an *eschatological* perspective. From the perspective of faith, the church must be understood in light of its future, as a sign and an anticipation of the fellowship between God and humans that will be brought about by the coming kingdom of God. Statements about the church as one and holy must not be understood as statements about an invisible church behind the visible, but about the church in light of its eschatological destiny.

12. Healy, *Church,* p. 66.

13. Miroslav Volf, *After Our Likeness: The Church as the Image of the Trinity* (Grand Rapids: Eerdmans, 1998), p. 136.

14. These questions are further discussed in Harald Hegstad, *The Real Church: An Ecclesiology of the Visible* (Eugene, OR: Pickwick Publications, forthcoming).

This understanding does not make the community of those gathering in the name of Jesus anything less than a human community. It is rather this concrete coming together of believers and the practices they engage in that constitute the church. As such the church is a social reality, accessible for empirical investigation. This points to the local church as the primary field for empirical studies, as well as for practical theology and for ecclesiology in a systematic-theological context.

Priorities of the local church do not exclude an interest in the church in its global or universal sense. Nor should this dimension of the church be understood as a nonempirical, purely ideal reality. The one universal church exists rather as a communion of churches, a communion that also may and should be described and examined empirically — and interpreted theologically.

The Necessity of Empirical Research on the Church

The understanding of the real church as an empirical reality means that the church should be investigated with all available methods and perspectives, especially those offered by the social sciences (because the church is a social phenomenon!). Such research should be undertaken by the social sciences themselves (results from such research should be critically evaluated by theology), and by theology itself. Without the use of social-scientific methods and perspectives, theology tends to make use of ideologically formed stereotypes when describing the church, based on limited personal experience. Implicit and explicit pictures of the church used by theology should be based on unbiased descriptions based on all the available data.

The use of social-scientific methods in the description of the church should not lead to a de-theologized ecclesiological language, but rather the opposite: theological statements regarding the church are statements about the empirical church! Ecclesiology should not limit itself to statements of the church in general, but should interpret the concrete existence of the church in a given context. This should lead to a richer theological understanding of the empirical church.

To understand the congregation as a local system, ecclesiology should make use of the available sociological perspectives and methods, both quantitative and qualitative. An important reminder from a sociological perspective is that the congregation should never be understood as a closed system, but as a system interacting with the broader society of which it is a part.[15]

A theological use of sociology should include the use of sociology's critical and revealing function, including revealing and criticizing power structures. The church is called to truth, also in its description of the situation. Theology should confirm what Peter Berger calls the "humanizing" function of sociology.[16]

Empirical and sociological perspectives on the church should not only be a matter for the researcher, but should also be included in the perspectives of the reflective practitioner. Such perspectives should thus be included in education for church ministry, providing ministers with methodological tools and theoretical perspectives for understanding congregations.

A Norwegian Case: The Double Social Structure of the Church

To illustrate the need for empirical research of the church, and of theological interpretation of the results from such research, I will present some perspectives from my own research on Norwegian church life. The following is built on ethnographic research in several congregations within the Church of Norway.

Judging from membership statistics, Norway seems to be a rather "churched" society, as 84 percent of the population are members of Christian churches. Out of these, 79 percent are members of the dominant church, the (Lutheran) Church of Norway, 5 percent of other churches (2010).[17] The adherence to the church is also manifested in a rather high level of participation in church rituals. Most church members bring their newborn children for baptism (70 percent of all newborn children in 2008), a majority of young people are confirmed in the church (66 percent of all fifteen-year-olds), and more than nine out of ten funerals are conducted in the church (93 percent).[18]

---

15. This is convincingly demonstrated in Nancy Ammerman, *Congregation and Community* (New Brunswick, NJ: Rutgers University Press, 1997).

16. Peter L. Berger, *The Sacred Canopy: Elements of a Sociological Theory of Religion* (New York: Doubleday, 1967), p. 8.

17. Numbers are based on data from *Årbok for Den norske kirke 2010* (Oslo: Kirkerådet, 2010), p. 75, and http://www.ssb.no. Only 2.5 percent are members of non-Christian communities.

18. *Årbok for Den norske kirke 2010*, p. 75 (all numbers are from 2008).

The picture is rather different when it comes to regular participation. At an ordinary Sunday service, only a small minority is present. In surveys, approximately 8 percent of the church members report that they go to church at least once a month, only 2 percent every week.[19] The church is at the same time a majority and a minority phenomenon!

As a majority phenomenon, the church is usually characterized as a "folk church" (Norwegian: "folkekirke"; German "Volkskirche"). As such, it serves as a social and ritual framework for people's religiosity. On the other hand, the church is an arena for active participation and personal commitment for a smaller group of believers. In some congregations, this group has a more semi-independent status in relation to the official church organization, and is often associated with the pietistic lay movement and local prayer houses. In other congregations, it is more integrated as a "core congregation." In some congregations, the distinction between those inside and outside this core is rather sharp (especially in contexts influenced by a revivalist context); in other congregations, the distinction is rather blurred.

The relation between these two social forms of church has been a subject of heavy debate in the Norwegian context. This debate has been characterized by an unclear relation between the understanding of the empirical phenomenon itself and the theological interpretation of it. Often theological evaluations have presupposed a one-sided understanding of the situation, which has been used to support a certain theological interpretation. In this situation an empirical, ethnographic type of research has proved itself fruitful in order to establish a more nuanced and comprehensive understanding of the situation. It has also contributed to a necessary distinction between the understanding of the phenomenon on an empirical level, and the theological interpretation of it — even if it is never possible to make a complete separation of the two.

In several ethnographic studies on local Norwegian congregations I have especially focused on analyzing the relation between the two social forms of the church described above. The aim has been to get an understanding of the complexity of the Norwegian folk church. Through qualitative observation and document analysis, the complex social and cultural configuration of Norwegian congregations has been described.[20]

19. Ida Marie Høeg, Harald Hegstad, and Ole Gunnar Winsnes, *Folkekirke 2000. En spørreundersøkelse blant medlemmer av Den norske kirke* (Oslo: Stiftelsen kirkeforskning, 2000), p. 43 (question 12).

20. Cf. Harald Hegstad, *Folkekirke og trosfellesskap* (Trondheim: Tapir, 1996); Harald

One possible perspective is to understand this complex situation as two forms of religiosity living side by side within the same church. This has been described by Oskar Skarsaune as the relation between temple religion and synagogue religion.[21] In the synagogue there is a congregation meeting for their common worship of God. In the temple there is no congregation, only individuals coming at different times to the sanctuary to bring forth their prayers and offerings. According to Skarsaune, churches in the Norwegian context may be understood as synagogues and temples at the same time — a place where the synagogue congregation meets for their service, and the temple visitor comes to have important rituals done (e.g., the baptism of a child). From a phenomenological point of view it thus can be argued that the church embodies two types of religion side by side.

In the ethnographic material this difference can be seen with regard to both religious self-understanding and practice. The difference in self-understanding is for instance reflected in the popular distinction between "ordinary Christians" and "personal" or "confessing Christians." The difference in practice is for instance reflected in the ambiguity in the use of the sacraments and other church ceremonies: The vast majority of church members baptize their children, making use of church confirmation for their youth and church burial for their dead. Only a minority of the church members participate in Holy Communion. Also, weekly church attendance is a minority phenomenon. For the majority of the church members going to church needs a specific "reason." The material thus shows two ways of being a church member and a Christian, each with its own pattern and logic. Whether or not there is a sharp dividing line between these alternatives, they vary according to local traditions and circumstances. An important factor for such local variations is to what degree revivalist traditions have been influential in the local church.

As striking as the differences are the *connection* and *interdependence* of these two ways of being a church member and a Christian. Even if they

---

Hegstad and Tore Laugerud, *Brennende hjerter eller misjonerende menigheter?* (Trondheim: Tapir, 2002); Harald Hegstad, Anne Schanche Selbekk, and Olaf Aagedal, *Når tro skal læres. Sju fortellinger om lokal trosopplæring* (Trondheim: Tapir, 1998). Results from the first study are reported in English in Harald Hegstad, "A Minority within the Majority: On the Relation between the Church as Folk Church and as a Community of Believers," *Studia Theologica* 53 (1999): 119-31.

21. Oskar Skarsaune, "Noen overveielser om norsk folkereligiøsitet," *Halvårsskrift for praktisk teologi* 10, no. 2 (1993): 13-18.

in some way oppose and exclude each other, they are at the same time elements within the same social system. On the one hand *the active core group presupposes the wider folk church.* It presupposes it as a cultural framework that is often taken for granted, but still is constitutive also for this group. This framework includes moral values; components of a worldview; elements of the biblical narrative etcetera present in common culture. It also presupposes the folk church by being itself part of the folk church. These people are using the same church rituals as other church members (e.g., infant baptism and church funerals). On these occasions they are even acting together with folk-church members who do not belong to the core group. They are recruited from the mass of ordinary church members, and they have this position as a place of refuge when leaving the group of active believers. One does not have to change religion when going from the one position to the other. It all happens within the same religion.

On the other hand, the active core group has *a maintaining function vis-à-vis the folk church.* It is maintaining the folk church through its active contribution to society and church life. The presence and efforts of active church members contribute to the upholding of the Christian element in the society, which is necessary also in order to uphold a folk church. Through their presence and contribution in the church, they are maintaining a church organization and a church life that are necessary if the church should function not only for its active members, but also as a folk church. The core group plays an important role in upholding Sunday services through their participation, and in upholding Christian knowledge and identity among the church members through their work with Sunday school and other Christian activities.

The core group does not only have a practical function, but also a symbolic and representative function in relation to the folk church. Originally this function belonged, and still belongs, to the minister/priest as the person representing the holy. The minister, however, often shares this function with a wider group that is associated with the church and with an active Christian commitment. The function of the minister and of the core group vis-à-vis the folk church explains the ambivalence that can be found among the ordinary church members toward this group. On the one hand they are important and necessary for one's one religious self-understanding, as symbol bearers and representative figures. On the other hand they are in a way a threat, a reminder that one does not believe and live according to the standards of the church in every respect. Therefore one values ministers and other religious representatives that are not "judging," but are ready to include and be tolerant. At the same time it is a shock and a scandal when ministers and other religious representatives act contrary to certain moral standards. Even if one is not living according to these standards oneself, it is good to know that at least someone (some religious symbol bearers) does. When they do not, that shakes the foundations.

This last aspect may function as ethnographic example of what Grace Davie names the "vicarious" element in modern European religiosity. Although the influence of churches is reduced and regular churchgoers comprise a minority of the population, they still fulfill an important function of maintaining the tradition on behalf of the majority.[22]

Theological Implications of the Ethnographic Analysis

The questions raised by this situation are not only sociological questions, but also theological ones. In a theological perspective it is necessary to ask for the theological, ecclesiological interpretation and evaluation of this picture. How can this be understood as a *church*, as the body of Christ? Which social form of the church is the church in a qualified sense: the broader folk church (the 79 percent) or the group of people actively involved with the church on a regular basis (the 10 percent)?

In the Norwegian context, there have traditionally been two alternative and opposing ecclesiological traditions. One tradition has understood the folk church as the real church, stressing the sacramental character of the church: the church simply is the baptized members, without regard to their level of activity or expression of belief. Another tradition has understood the core group as the real church, stressing the church's character as a community of believers. The folk church is in this perspective an important context for evangelism.

An interesting aspect is that each of these theological traditions has had its own interpretation of the situation in sociological terms. The folk church tradition has traditionally been quite optimistic regarding the role of Christian faith in the lives of ordinary church members. The other tradition has interpreted this situation rather negatively, talking about "nominal membership" etc.

22. Grace Davie, *Religion in Modern Europe: A Memory Mutates* (Oxford: Oxford University Press, 2000).

In my experience, a nuanced description of the situation, based on empirical research, has contributed to a more fruitful theological debate in this field. Showing the complexity and ambiguity of the situation makes clear-cut theological evaluations more difficult. The complexity of the situation should also be taken into account when it comes to a theological interpretation and evaluation. This means that there can be no simple choice between identifying the church as the folk church group and the core group. They are both aspects of the church from a theological perspective. As indicated above, the point of departure in the theological understanding of the church is the gathering in the name of Jesus (in a Lutheran terminology: around word and sacrament). This cannot mean that the church is restricted to those who are actually gathering at a given moment. This would cause the church to cease existing when it is not gathered. To belong to the church is to have a relation to this gathering. Every baptized person has some relation to this gathering, as she was once baptized in this setting. At the same time, the church needs someone who is actually gathering on a regular basis — in order to stay a church. Thus the sociological concept of vicarious religiosity may also be given a theological interpretation.

This should not be understood as a harmonizing description. To be a church member just by showing up a few times during a lifespan is certainly a shadowy form of church membership. A theological perspective should not be limited to interpretation, but should also lead to some directions for development. Also, a folk church in terms of its ecclesiology should be understood as a missional ecclesiology.

My intention is not to go deep into this question, but to use it as an illustration of the points I made in the first part of this chapter. If the task of theological ecclesiology is not primarily to interpret the ideal church but the concrete church in all its messiness, it will have to engage in empirical research on the church in the specific social contexts where it is found. Such data are not to be understood as illustrations or fields of applications of a-contextual theological insights; they should rather be understood as a source for theological reflection.

This does not mean that ecclesiological reflection is limited to one context at a time. Even if the attempt of a theological interpretation also of the not-so-active members of the church stems from the specific folk church situation, it may also challenge theological reflections in other contexts, where the church tends to be identified with its active members. A theology of the church that is open for the diverse reality of the church has to engage in empirical research on the church in its complexity.

On Congregations and Worship

CHAPTER 3

Affirming Faith at a Service of Baptism in St. Aldates Church, Oxford

Paul S. Fiddes and Pete Ward

The Service Observed

We are presenting a study of a service of adult baptism and renewal of baptismal vows in water, held at St. Aldates Church in Oxford (Church of England) on Pentecost Sunday 2009. We attended the service, and our study is also based on a detailed review of video recordings made both by ourselves and by St. Aldates, used by permission of the leaders of the church.

As one enters the church, there is a very impressive new vestibule with a "welcome desk" and a group of four or five people ready to greet visitors and give them a leaflet containing the notices for the week. Parts of the church date from the Norman period, although Nikolaus Pevsner rather gloomily observes that most of the current buildings are a result of remodeling carried out by Canon Christopher in the latter half of the nineteenth century.[1] In more recent times the body of the church has undergone even more substantial reordering, as it is now carpeted, with large numbers of contemporary-style plain wood and metal chairs arranged in sections around a raised platform. The platform is mainly taken up with the equipment for the worship band. It is a curious see-through construction resembling an upturned fish tank; it contains a drum kit, and when the worship gets going it becomes clear that this device is a baffle to control the sound produced by the drummer. At the front of the platform

---

1. Jennifer Sherwood and Nikolaus Pevsner, *Oxfordshire* (Harmondsworth, UK: Penguin, 1974), p. 287.

there is a perspex lectern. To the right there is a baptistry large enough for the total immersion of adult believers; at the beginning of the service the rector, Charlie Cleverly, jokingly refers to it as "the Jacuzzi." Around each of the pillars in the church are audio speakers for the PA system and two or three large TV screens, airport style. There is a large banner hanging on the wall to the left of the stage. The banner has a picture of the earth taken from space and in large letters it declares "My house will be called a house of prayer for the nations."

The service began at 6:00 p.m. and lasted for a little over an hour and a half, attended by six hundred people. A summary of the service, as observed, is as follows.

Before the Service. The church is filled with a buzz of conversation as the seats fill up. On the TV screens a short film is being played showing large numbers of people gathering in what appears to be a football stadium somewhere in Africa; it is difficult to make out what is happening, and most of the congregation are paying it no attention.

The Welcome. With no introduction the rector gets up from a seat in the congregation and picks up a microphone from the lectern. He is wearing a short-sleeve shirt with a tie. He says, "Good evening and welcome to St. Aldates" and then explains that we have been watching a video for the Global Day of Prayer, where "hundreds of thousands of Christians across the time zones will be praying that God will do a new thing in his creation." He explains that this is significant because today is the Day of Pentecost. He reads from Acts 2 and then emphasizes that as the disciples gathered, tongues of flame came to rest upon them. "So watch out," he warns the congregation.

Confession. A prayer of confession appears on the TV screens and the rector leads the congregation in saying this together. The confession comes from the Church of England *Common Worship,* "An Order for Night Prayer (Compline)."[2]

Absolution. The rector reads a prayer of absolution from the TV screen. The text is taken from *Common Worship,* "Authorized Forms of Confession and Absolution."[3]

Praise. Four songs follow: "How Great Thou Art," "Come Hear the Thunder of a Victory Cry," "There Is a Redeemer," and "Fire Fall Down."

2. *Common Worship: Services and Prayers for the Church of England* (London: Church House Publishing, 2000), p. 81.

3. *Common Worship,* pp. 135-37.

The songs are sung by a male worship leader who plays a low-slung acoustic guitar. The band consists of bass, keyboards, drums, and two female backup singers. The style is Indie Rock. All the songs are run together so that one song merges with the next.

Prayer. The rector prays an extempore prayer. He asks that God will send his fire as a symbol of his presence. He speaks of times when revival has come in the past, recalling how in Oxford there have been times of revival. He says that "we are praying for that in our land in this season." He prays for any in the congregation who are needy, thirsty, or in need of healing. He asks for God who is the truth and the life to send blessing "in this season."

The Peace. After the prayer there is a moment for sharing "the Peace." The rector asks people to express the spirit of Pentecost when we were made all one family. He says, "The peace of the Lord be always with you"; the liturgical response, "and also with you," is not displayed on the screen and it is mumbled by the congregation. The rector then invites the congregation to turn around and say hello to someone near to them. Everyone does this with general enthusiasm, and some lengthy conversations ensue.

The Notices. The rector invites us to look at the screens, and a video appears called "The Essentials." These are the weekly notices for St. Aldates. Each notice is intended to appear as a short commercial with music, dancing, TV-friendly reporters, and head-and-shoulders quotes from key leaders. The adverts are for the following: (1) Postgraduate Students Group — who do a rap song; (2) the revamped Catacombs Prayer rooms, where Oxford Christian leaders give their support and are shown writing prayers on the wall so that "in the very foundations it will be a house of prayer"; (3) a women's meeting on the subject of depression; (4) "Mighty Warriors" children's party; (5) a mission trip to Mozambique; (6) a newcomers' welcome lunch at St. Aldates. Unfortunately, the video system stops working in the third item, and the audience can only hear the sound.

Explanation of Baptism. The curate comes to the lectern and picks up the handheld microphone. He is wearing a white shirt with a tie and jeans. He introduces the baptismal liturgy by explaining that baptism is a time when we get "really excited about what God has done for us through Jesus." We make serious promises, and it is a time when we make the beginning of our faith journey that goes on for the rest of our lives. We are welcomed by the church, whose members promise to love us and support us and "stand alongside us and pray for us." Baptism, he says, is full of beautiful imagery of dying and rising with Christ, of being washed and being signed with the cross on our foreheads.[4] The curate then explains that each candidate will come forward and "tell us a little bit about their journey"; they will then be fully immersed, and after this friends and family are invited to gather round them while they are in the pool and pray for them.

Baptism Liturgy. The curate leads the congregation and the candidates in a shortened form of the baptismal liturgy from "Holy Baptism" in the Church of England's *Common Worship,* selecting texts and reordering them. First he invites the candidates and the whole congregation to affirm their faith, "to show that we believe in one faith," using a responsive text projected on the TV screens. This is an alternative version of the "Profession of Faith" provided in *Common Worship* (headed "to be used where there are strong pastoral reasons").[5] The responses are made enthusiastically. The curate then asks the candidates the series of questions that stand under the heading "Decision" in *Common Worship* (beginning "In baptism God calls us out of darkness into his marvellous light"),[6] to which the candidates respond by affirming their resolve to repent of sin and turn to Christ.

Testimonies and Baptism. Each candidate comes to the platform one by one. They take the microphone and give a short testimony concerning their journey of faith. Of the six candidates five are from Christian families, and nearly all speak of the "privilege" they had growing up in a Christian ethos. Three of the candidates declare that they will be renewing their baptismal vows, having been previously baptized as children. Nevertheless, all speak about an experience of radical change.

They then go to the baptismal pool where an unidentified male says their name and before immersing them backwards into the water says either, "on confession of faith I baptize you in the name of the Father, the Son and the Holy Spirit," or if they have been baptized already as an infant, "on confession of faith it is our pleasure to reaffirm your baptism vows in the name of the Father, the Son and the Holy Spirit." The immersions are shown on the screen, filmed by a handheld camera above the baptistry. Immediately following each immersion people rush up from the congregation and gather round the candidate, holding hands over the candidate or touching him or her and praying. As this takes place the next candidate comes to the lectern and picks up the microphone to give a testimony. The whole process seems to be very well rehearsed with no pauses.

4. In fact, signing with the cross is to be omitted in this particular service.
5. *Common Worship,* p. 373.
6. *Common Worship,* p. 353.

Songs and Offering. The band returns to the stage for two songs: "Oh Happy Day" and "I Am a Friend of God." Before the songs start, the curate invites us to stand and explains that there will be a collection, but he asks visitors not to feel that they should give anything. As the songs are sung collection plates are passed around; there is no offertory prayer.

Sermon. The rector goes to the lectern and picks up the microphone, leading the clapping after the last song. The sermon starts with a short opening prayer asking for an openness to what the Bible says. He says that this sermon is part of a series on the book of Philippians, and, referring to the previous song, announces that later he will invite people to become "friends of God." This is Pentecost Sunday when the Spirit fell on the church. Around about him, he says, he sees a world that is groaning: the economy is collapsing and we are disintegrating morally and we are longing for the leadership of Jesus Christ. There is then a reading from Philippians 2:1-13, read by the rector, and he intersperses the reading with short explanatory additions. The sermon follows a two-part structure. The first and by far the lengthiest section asks the congregation to "consider Christ." The rector argues for Christ's uniqueness and continued significance, drawing less directly on the Gospel narrative than on the words of a number of historical and theological figures who have regarded Christ highly. With this apologetic he moves to explain the significance of the cross. Here he uses an illustration, familiar in evangelistic preaching, of two hands and the Bible. The one hand represents humanity and the Bible represents a barrier between humanity and God. He then passes the Bible over to the other hand and explains that the barrier of sin is laid on Christ so we can have fellowship with God. The second section of the sermon deals with Christ-likeness. The rector sets down a challenge to the church. There is no life in Christ without a likeness to Christ. From Philippians he talks about leadership that "goes down low." It is this kind of leadership that is needed, both in the church and in society. "In this season, in this time," he says, "we are witnessing the collapse of Christian civilization as we know it." What we need is a willingness to accept downward mobility if we are to embrace the call to serve Christ.

Prayer and Song. The rector leads a short prayer. He asks people to sing "Receive Our Adoration" and says, "I sense a prayerful atmosphere."

Prophetic Word. The rector invites one of the members to give a short message. He says that while the rector was speaking the Lord gave him a Bible verse from Acts 2 where Peter at the day of Pentecost quotes the Old Testament prophecy in which God says, "I will pour out my Spirit on all

55

flesh." He says that he asked God why he was being given this verse at this time and the Lord said that it is for those who "Go down low." These will be the ones who are filled with the Spirit. Notably, this word links Pentecost with the theme of the sermon.

Invitation and Ministry Time. While the organ plays quietly the rector says, "If that's you and you want more of the Holy Spirit, come up to the front." He invites those who are being called to "go down low and be filled with the Spirit" to come forward, either to receive Christ for the first time or to commit to servant leadership. He explains that every week at St. Aldates they do this. He then asks the ministry team to come forward and "bless what God is doing."

Blessing. While people are coming forward and they are being prayed for, the rector gives a general blessing, saying, "The Blessing of God Almighty, Father Son and Holy Spirit the Comforter will reach into every heart in this room tonight and always."

Final Words. Charlie announces that "the Spirit of the Lord is here" and people should feel free to "linger" in his presence. At this point he says "welcome back" to the candidates for baptism and renewal of baptismal vows (they have been changing after their immersion in water). There is loud applause. He then asks the congregation to leave quickly because there is another service due to start at 8:15 p.m. People start to chat as they slowly leave and all the while the prayer at the front by the platform continues.

Four Merging Currents in the Performance of Worship

Evangelicalism is generally seen as a conservative form of Christianity with clearly defined boundaries and doctrinal formulations. David Bebbington for instance defines evangelicalism through a much-quoted, and indeed critiqued, summary of four key distinctives: conversionism, activism, Biblicism, and crucicentrism.[7] Each of these elements is there at St. Aldates but what this kind of definition does not capture is the way that charismatic expression is formed from the merging of several streams of theology, liturgy, and culture. At St. Aldates these streams are seen to be moving with, and in and out of, one another in the performance of worship.

---

7. David Bebbington, *Evangelicalism in Modern Britain: A History from the 1730s to the 1980s* (London: Unwin, 1989), p. 3.

The Anglican Liturgy

There are three elements of the worship that make direct use of Anglican liturgy: the confession, the absolution, and selections from the liturgy of Baptism. In addition to this the final blessing also shows a sensibility that could be read as coming from an Anglican tradition. The performance of liturgy is distinctive in this evangelical setting because it requires the congregation to say a set pattern of words together in unison. Although the service begins with a corporate prayer of confession, the "Affirmation of Faith" that begins the baptismal liturgy comes as a kind of formal interruption in what has been a very informal service since that opening point. The congregation is asked to "sign up" publicly to a set of beliefs by standing and making responses together, which end with the statement: "This is the faith of the church. This is our faith. We believe and trust in one God, Father, Son, and Holy Spirit."[8]

It is interesting that St. Aldates, as a charismatic church, feels that it should include these more formal elements. There is a self-conscious choice to include these aspects, which may come from a kind of residual Anglican identity and may also come from some notion of "compliance" with Anglican liturgical norms. Such a sensitivity to following Anglican rules may be particularly acute with regard to the sacraments, in this case the baptismal liturgy. At the same time the texts used in the worship have been chosen for their inclusion in a particular style of worship. The confession for instance comes from "An Order for Night Prayer," rather than from Evening Prayer. It may have been chosen because it is shorter, and for the appropriateness of the concluding words, "heal us by your Spirit and raise us to new life in Christ." Similarly the absolution has been selected from a group of optional prayers. The "Affirmation of Faith" used in the baptismal liturgy is an alternative provided to the one set in the main text, and consists of a series of affirmations read by the leader with a short response from the congregation ("I believe and trust in him") rather than the usual corporate saying of the Apostles' Creed. Most notably, the selection from the baptismal liturgy omits three important elements in *Common Worship*, of which we shall have more to say later: the signing with the cross,[9] the "Prayer over the Water,"[10] and the section called "Commission."[11]

8. *Common Worship*, p. 373.
9. *Common Worship*, p. 354.
10. *Common Worship*, p. 355.
11. *Common Worship*, pp. 358-59.

The liturgy introduces significant doctrinal elements, and in particular a deeply ingrained trinitarian formulation, into the worship at St. Aldates. At the same time the chosen elements are homologous with the other elements that make up the merging currents in St. Aldates' worship. The repetition of believing and trusting in God in the alternative "Affirmation of Faith" supports and sustains the evangelical ethos, as do the responses made by the candidates, which speak of repentance of sins and turning to Christ. This evangelical sensibility is also evident in the choice of confession and absolution as the only other key liturgical elements, items that are not actually part of the *Common Worship* order for baptism at all. Together these elements suggest a journey of conversion that is being revisited. At the same time the language of "trust" as well as belief and "submitting to Christ" and also the references to the "devil" and renouncing "evil" in the candidates' chosen responses have resonances with charismatic and revivalist theology.

Conservative Evangelicalism

St. Aldates is a charismatic church but it is also evangelical in its history and its tradition. This is seen four main ways. First, *the Bible is prominent.* The rector reads from Acts 2 right at the start of the service to explain the Christian origins of the festival of Pentecost. Then at the start of the sermon he reads a section from Philippians, and the full text is displayed on the screens so the congregation can read along with him. The Bible, it is clear, is to be the focus of the preaching not just this week but all through the university term, when there is a sermon series on Philippians, preaching on every chapter. So in common with many evangelical churches, preaching is structured around sequential series working through a book from the Bible rather than making use of the lectionary.

As well as an emphasis on the Bible, the service shows, second, a continual commitment to *an evangelical emphasis on conversion.* The baptismal testimonies are presented as conversion narratives, drawing attention to how each individual became a follower of Christ. The first part of the sermon is designed to present Christ as the basis for life, and people are told that they will be invited to become Christians. The opening prayer also makes it clear that the service is a place where those who are hungry and thirsty can find comfort and healing. Third, the preaching of the cross as *penal substitution* is a characteristic of the evangelical presentation of the "gospel." When the rector uses the illustration with the Bible, and transfers it to the hand that represents Christ, he uses the words "and the Lord has laid on him the iniquity of us all." These words and actions reveal a theological pedigree that links present-day charismatics to evangelicals of previous generations.[12]

Finally, the evangelical roots of St. Aldates are seen in the *style of singing*. Although the music that the church uses is drawn from contemporary charismatic worship, it is interesting that nowhere in the songs is space made for "intimacy."[13] "Intimacy" here refers to quieter moments of reflection and prayer. Charismatic songs often have a structure of crescendo and diminuendo, and as the volume of the singing becomes much less people pray either in tongues or silently. The songs at St. Aldates, in contrast, are almost entirely "upbeat" in nature. They are therefore much closer to the kind of "hearty singing" that characterized the previous era of evangelical song.[14]

The Charismatic Style

The style of singing at the service has elements from an evangelical culture, but there are also significant aspects that draw on mainstream charismatic style and performance. Around the church at various points people are seen to have their arms held in the air. The worship leader uses the characteristic technique of repeating elements of the songs and shouting over the top of the singing such phrases as "Yes Lord!"

Charismatic worship, however, is more evident in the way that the

12. The same illustration is used by Nicky Gumbel in the Alpha Course; *Alpha* (Eastbourne, UK: Kingsway Publications, 1993), p. 61, probably dating right back to R. A. Torrey; see Torrey, *Personal Work* (repr. London: Pickering & Inglis, 1974), p. 3. In 1912 Torrey led an influential mission for the newly formed Cambridge Inter-Collegiate Christian Union; see Douglas Johnson, *Contending for the Faith: A History of the Evangelical Movement in the Universities and Colleges* (Leicester, UK: Inter-Varsity Press, 1979), p. 78. A few years later the same illustration with the Bible was used by the founder of Iwerne Minster Camps, Eric Nash (Bash); see Dick Knight, "The Speaker," in *Bash: A Study in Spiritual Power*, ed. John Eddison (Basingstoke, UK: Marshalls, 1982), p. 50. "Bash Camps," as they were known, nurtured the theological sensibilities of generations of evangelical leaders; see Pete Ward, *Growing Up Evangelical: Youthwork and the Making of a Subculture* (London: SPCK 1996), pp. 36-51.

13. See Pete Ward, *Selling Worship* (Milton Keynes, UK: Paternoster, 2006), p. 202.

14. Ward, *Selling Worship*, p. 200.

Holy Spirit is invoked. The rector twice uses the phrase "Come Holy Spirit." He does this right at the start of the service between the confession and the absolution, echoing the phrase "heal us by your spirit" at the end of the confession. The opening prayer also follows this theme, referring to the fire coming down from heaven at the Day of Pentecost. Then at the end of the service when people come forward the rector announces "The Spirit of the Lord is here." This kind of invocation was introduced to the UK through the ministry of John Wimber and was then popularized through the New Wine and Soul Survivor networks. At St. Aldates the invocation of the Spirit is accompanied by another characteristic Wimber innovation, "the ministry team." At the service when people are coming forward, the rector asks the ministry team to come forward also and "bless what God is doing." This notion of blessing alongside intercessory prayer is also seen in the prayer for the candidates while they are in the pool. Here people are seen to hold their hands a few inches (or in some cases because of the pool a foot or two) away from the person's head or body while praying. This practice is again one that was made common in the 1980s through the conferences led by John Wimber.

Revivalism

Alongside the charismatic elements drawn from Wimber and the New Wine movements at St. Aldates there is another distinctive theology. This we term "revivalism," and it is most closely associated with the rector, Charlie Cleverly, himself. A characteristic of this theological element in the worship is the phrase "in this season." This phrase is used by the rector frequently. It is there in the opening prayer, when he says, "We pray that you will send your blessing in this season, in this time." It is repeated in the sermon where "in this season" is linked to "in this prophetic time." (The phrase "in this season" also appears on the St. Aldates website.) The notion of a season or a prophetic time is linked to the sense that God is doing or about to do a new thing. This theme is introduced right at the start of the service when the rector speaks about the video that has been playing as people come into the church. The Global Day of Prayer, he explains, is when hundreds of thousands of Christians are praying "that God would come and do a new thing in his creation." Again in the introduction the rector says that he is excited about what God is doing "in this time." Explicit reference is made to revival in the opening prayer. Here he speaks about the prayerful expectation that revival will return to "this land" and in particular in "our own city of Oxford." He says, "People have sought your face and revival has come to nations. We are praying for that in our land in this season."

The language of "our land," "this season," and "the nations" introduces an apocalyptic element into the worship, and this is associated with a pessimism concerning society and also the wider church. In the sermon the need for revival is linked to a world that is seen as groaning and disintegrating morally. The rector speaks about the present time as a "winter that will soon be over," a time when the "temporary madness that is over our city will soon be over."

Theological Reflection: Participating in God

We have seen how four currents of theology and culture flow together into the ethos of worship in this service. There is a fluidity about this construct: different strands coexist, and the remains of previous movements of Christian life and mission are still visible in the mixture. We now want to make a theological inquiry into the way that this mingling of elements helps, or perhaps hinders, the *participation* in the triune God that is at the heart of true worship.

In worship we do not contemplate the three persons of the Trinity as if they were three supernatural beings, not even as an exercise in our minds. We do not *observe* God, but we *participate* in the divine fellowship as God opens up the divine life to make room for us to dwell. Taking a clue from Augustine and Aquinas who, in different cultural contexts, proposed that "the [divine] names refer to the relations"[15] or "person signifies relation,"[16] we may suggest that talk of "persons" in God is nothing less than a language of relationships, and "Trinity" only makes sense as we actually participate in these movements of relation.[17] We share in an interweaving of sacrificial movements of giving and receiving that we can only say are like relationships between a father and a son, or a mother and a daughter, opened up to new depths of love and turned to a new hope in the future by

15. Augustine, *De Trinitate* 5.6.

16. Aquinas, *Summa Theologiae* 1a.29.4.

17. See Paul S. Fiddes, *Participating in God: A Pastoral Doctrine of the Trinity* (London: Darton, Longman & Todd, 2000), pp. 34-50, 81-86.

an energetic flow that we can only call "Spirit." One way of describing these movements is a Trinity of sending: as the Father sends forth the Son on mission into the world in the power of the Spirit, we can share in being sent. Another description is a Trinity of glory: the Father displays his glory in the Son, the Son glorifies the Father in a Spirit of transformation, and as we share in praise to the Father we ourselves are changed from glory to glory.[18] Nor ought we to miss a Trinity of suffering: our own suffering which so often seems senseless is given meaning as we share in worship in a movement of suffering that is like a Father losing a Son and a Son abandoned by a Father in a Spirit of self-surrender and empathy.

Now, from this theological perspective, how well does the mingling of four elements in this service of baptism enable us to share in the relations between Father, Son, and Holy Spirit?

Turning first to the remaining presence of Anglican liturgy, we have observed that elements have been selected that will support the aspect of "witness to faith" in conservative evangelicalism. This stresses our willing participation in God, but we will not be properly enabled to participate unless we notice the movements of *God* that are calling and drawing us into deeper engagement with the fellowship of God's own life, in sending, glorifying, and suffering. Here we miss the content of the "prayer over the water," however it might be expressed, in which God's own actions in creation and salvation history are recalled here and now in baptism. In the prayer provided in *Common Worship* there is an appeal to the Holy Spirit who "moved in the beginning of creation," that those baptized "may be cleansed from sin and born again." The prayer asks God the Father, that "[r]enewed in your image [they] may walk by the light of faith and continue forever in the risen life of Jesus Christ our Lord."[19] By choosing the mode of baptism by full immersion, the church has rightly wanted to take advantage of a sacramental action that in itself enables the participation of the whole physical body in the movement of God's life, since God immerses God's very self into human sin, death, and nothingness in the dying of Christ on the cross, and triumphs over them all. However, we notice that the liturgical words are missing that can comment on the act, and being addressed to God in prayer, can help to draw those baptized into God's own activity for human renewal.

18. For the Trinity of sending and glorification, see Jürgen Moltmann, *The Church in the Power of the Spirit*, trans. M. Kohl (London: SCM, 1977), pp. 53-56, 57-60.

19. *Common Worship*, p. 355.

Similarly, the conservative-evangelical stress on Scripture is seen in the use of Scripture as a text for study and preaching during the sermon, underlined by its display on the TV screens at this point. But no Scripture is attached to the act of baptism, to interpret it and to be a means of God's own speaking and summoning the candidates and congregation more deeply into God's life.

The charismatic elements in the worship have their own way of fostering participation, and to some extent they provide a kind of sacramental sensibility that would otherwise be lacking in this conservative-evangelical ethos. Moving in the rhythm of the music during the singing, coming to the baptistry to pray and hold hands over the candidates, and coming forward in response to the "appeal" at the end all witness to a sharing in the movement of God's life. The gathering of friends around the candidates at the baptismal pool and the outstretching of hands is a climactic moment in which disciples of Christ can share in the outpouring of God's grace; the act has a "sacramental" feel to it, engaging the senses directly in contrast to prayer at a distance. In particular, the "appeal," combining an evangelical invitation to accept Christ with a charismatic offer of prayer ministry, provides an opportunity to participate with the whole body in the missionary movement of God. Those coming forward to kneel are invited by the rector to participate in the humble movement of "coming down low" that Christ has made, with the expectation of receiving new life through the Holy Spirit. The "word of prophecy" links the evangelical stress on following Christ with the charismatic element of being filled with the Spirit.

Nevertheless, we notice that there is no connection made between this moment of "coming down low" and the "coming down low" of baptism by immersion. Nor, in the act of baptism itself, is any reference made to receiving in baptism the gifts of the Spirit for sharing in God's mission ("sending") in the world. It is as if the sacramental aspects of baptism are being relocated into a new ritual, leaving baptism simply as a profession of faith, despite the reference in the introductory explanation to dying and rising with Christ. Implicitly, the service does provide an opportunity, with its concluding rite, for all those present to participate in the movement of baptism along with the candidates, but this opportunity could have been more effectively presented if the baptismal rite itself had also been explicitly seen as a ministry of God to the candidates.

One of the advantages of baptizing those who can profess faith for themselves, rather than as very young infants, is the opportunity for "ordaining" or commissioning disciples for service in the world, and so for their being equipped by God with gifts of the Spirit. The theme of commissioning is present in *Common Worship* in the section called "Commission" (omitted at St. Aldates), and filling with the Spirit is referred to in such phrases as "daily be renewed by his anointing Spirit"[20] and "bring forth the fruit of the Spirit."[21] However, the theme of the Spirit is muted in *Common Worship* baptism, probably because baptism in the Anglican rite is separated from confirmation with its act of laying on hands with the invocation: "Let your Holy Spirit rest upon them."[22] The separation is due, of course, to the traditional practice of the baptism of young infants, so that the process of initiation is — in their case — to be completed *later* in confirmation when they can profess faith for themselves. The separation between water baptism and receiving the Spirit ("baptism in Spirit")[23] persists when essentially the same order of baptism is used both for infants and "those who are able to answer for themselves."

At St. Aldates the concluding ritual does indeed offer an opportunity for the whole congregation to be "daily renewed with the anointing Spirit" (as the *Order for Baptism* puts it)[24] and to be commissioned for "servant leadership." However, the candidates for baptism and renewal of vows, though reappearing at the end of the service after changing their clothes, were not themselves explicitly included in this opportunity, which could easily have happened. Theologically, then, it would be good to have some joined-up thinking between the charismatic act of "coming down low in order to be to be filled" and baptism; indeed, baptism on Pentecost Sunday is the ideal moment for doing so. In this way all those present would be enabled to share more deeply in the movement of God who comes down low in order to "fill all things."

The element of revivalism also tends to detach the activity of God from baptism itself, though it need not do so. We have noted the revivalist stress on the expectation that God will "do a new thing," with the dramatic announcement that "this is the time and the season." Here the action of God tends to be pushed forward into the future, as an apocalyptic event

---

20. *Common Worship*, p. 357.

21. *Common Worship*, p. 359.

22. *Christian Initiation: Common Worship* (London: Church House Publishing, 2006), p. 118.

23. But, contrary to our argument, James Dunn argues for separation of "baptism in Spirit" from water baptism: *Baptism in the Holy Spirit* (London: SCM, 1970), pp. 31-37.

24. *Common Worship*, p. 357.

that will affect the nation in an imminent time to come. Yet theologically, baptism itself is a *kairos* moment, a turning-point in time when God does "a new thing": from their commissioning at this life-changing "time" disciples can begin to share in the establishing of God's kingdom, to participate in the divine movements of sending and being sent. This is truly the "season," but this particular baptismal service does not associate a "season of blessing" with baptism, and no connection is made between baptism and mission.

Apocalyptic expectations such as mark revivalism *can* detract from work for the kingdom here and now, but they can also give this a keener edge, overturning the mere status quo of the world with a confidence in God's ability to bring about a new creation.[25] In this service at St. Aldates a future event of renewal seems in fact to be *anticipated* in the filling of people by the Spirit in their response to the invitation. A commissioning through baptism could give content to this response in terms of discipleship in the contemporary world. The baptismal commissioning provided in *Common Worship* asks: "Will you acknowledge Christ's authority over human society, by prayer for the world and its leaders, by defending the weak, and by seeking peace and justice?"[26] Responding to this challenge will mean sharing in God's movement of mission in the wider world here and now, without losing either a sense of special prophetic "moments" or the conviction that the kingdom will not fully come until God brings about the reconciliation of all things.

The Performance of Worship: Mediation and Articulation

The eclectic theological and cultural strands that flow together into the performance of worship at St. Aldates are communicated with the use of a range of media. This mediated theological mix is in turn articulated in worship with the help of cultural elements; these include sociability, hospitality, and a self-consciousness about belonging in the university.

25. See Jürgen Moltmann, *The Future of Creation,* trans. M. Kohl (London: SCM Press, 1979), pp. 9-12.
26. *Common Worship,* p. 359.

Mediation: Visual Imagery and the Sound System

With contemporary worship music being so important in the service, the sound system and the various technical elements associated with a live band have a central place visually. Mention has already been made of the "fish tank" baffle that the drummer and his drum kit are encased in, and almost half of the platform area is taken up with the worship band and their equipment. There is no altar or communion table visible. The worship leader is standing in the middle of the stage behind the perspex lectern, and during the songs he sings into a microphone and adopts the stance of a rock singer at a concert. This rock-concert element is extended to applause following some of the songs. The sound system is an important signifier related to those leading the service: as the rector comes to the front of the platform it is when he picks up the large microphone that people start to become quiet. The microphone, because it is held in the hand, is also a key feature associated with everyone who comes to the lectern to speak.

Throughout the service the TV screens are used to display images, beginning with the scenes of prayer for revival, followed almost immediately by a liturgical text. For the notices these images take the form of short popular documentary-style reports advertising the events taking place at St. Aldates. The use of a TV style for the activities of the church not only locates the church as an exciting place in the flow of key events but also serves to connect faith with the discourse of popular television. The TV screens are also used to display the lyrics of the songs, and as the lyrics are shown there are moving images that act as the background to the words. These images are changed throughout the worship set. There are four main films used during the worship. The first is of a cross and the sky with clouds moving across it; the second is of a candle; the third shows the earth from space; the fourth shows a young man on a cliff with his arms raised in the air, while beneath him the sea is breaking on the cliff. The images correspond to the four elements of air, fire, earth, and water. This association is probably unintentional, but as with all aspects of mediation, be it the use of Indie Rock style in the worship songs, or the adoption of popular TV-style documentary for the notices, there are aspects of this contextualization that sit less than comfortably in a church setting. However, while the music carries mainly the strands of evangelical and charismatic worship, the TV screens are used to mediate all four elements.

Articulation: Sociability and Consciousness of Oxford

Throughout the service there is evidence that St. Aldates is a sociable church. Before the service begins, as the building starts to fill the noise level of people chatting and greeting each other begins to rise. At the Peace this cheerful buzz breaks out again as people introduce themselves to each other enthusiastically, and it is also there at the close of the service. St. Aldates appears to be a place to meet and to see people, and indeed it is a place to be seen. With six hundred people, mainly young adults, attending the evening service at 6:00 p.m. and with a similar number coming at 8:15 p.m. the social significance of the church cannot be underestimated. The importance of friendship is underlined by the references made to the role played by friends from St. Aldates by three of the six candidates for baptism and renewal of vows in their testimonies. The church fosters the sense of a hospitable welcome to a warm social gathering. The newly built entrance and the redeveloped graveyard with its paved area at the front of the church reinforce this kind of fellowship. At the close of the service, for instance, on what is a very hot evening, there are large crowds standing around talking to each other a good half hour after the service has ended, and the rector is observed sitting on a wall chatting to a couple of young worshipers.

There are many references to Oxford and the University throughout the service. In the sermon in particular the University motto *Dominus illuminatio mea,* "the Lord is my light," is cited. There is reference to Michael Green's much-quoted phrase among fellow-evangelicals that he came up to Oxford for a first, a blue, and a wife and achieved all three. (For those unfamiliar with Oxford customs, a "first" means a first-class degree and a "blue" is an award for representing Oxford against the University of Cambridge in sport.) Charlie adapts this to claim that he came up to Oxford to join a band, get high, and get into bed with a girl — although he does explain that he was not a Christian. He says he "won't tell the congregation" which of these he achieved but that the most important thing by far in coming to Oxford was for him, and is for him today, to find Christ. The reference to a blue, a first, and a boyfriend is also mentioned by one of the baptismal candidates. Much of the sermon appears directed towards reassuring the students present that they can be Christians and still be intellectually and socially respectable as Oxford students; here the predominant element seems to be a conservative-evangelical one, and is typical of teaching in the Christian Union in the University over many years.

Theological Reflection: The Performance

We have already drawn attention to the nature of the performance as giving little attention to the activity of God in baptism. This seems to be a result of the way that the different strands of tradition have been merged together — a selection from the Anglican liturgy to fit in with other elements, a disconnection of revivalist expectation from the event of baptism, a conservative-evangelical stress on "following Christ" in baptism, and a charismatic stress on receiving the Spirit outside baptism. We have also been sensitive to other ways in which the worship does positively encourage a participation in the activity of the triune God, and the huge *potential* the worship has for integrating baptism into these other forms of participation, which we suggest would lead to a deeper sharing in the mission of God. However, the lack of attention to what God is doing in baptism or in the baptismal waters seems to have two results in the style of the performance.

First, there is a curious lack of theology about the connection of the renewal of baptismal vows to the act of immersion in water. There is no need here to elaborate on the fact that the Liturgical Commission of the Church of England stresses that this practice, often dubbed "the New Zealand rite,"[27] should not be enacted in a way that gives any "appearance" of rebaptism.[28] Here we want only to comment on the formula used, which is: "On confession of faith it is our pleasure to reaffirm your baptism vows in the name of the Father, the Son, and the Holy Spirit." Without being overcritical, we must notice that the administrant declares "[we] reaffirm your baptism vows," while the whole point of the rite is for the *candidate* to "reaffirm" them. The church cannot do it. Others, including the church, made the vows vicariously in the first place, and it is now for the candidate to "reaffirm" them with his or her own profession of faith. What then

27. So called after its first use among congregations of the Presbyterian Church of Aotearoa, New Zealand. For an account of its reception in the General Assembly of the Church in 1977, see Samuel J. D. McCay, "Celebrating Renewal and Appropriation of Baptism by Immersion," in *Infant Baptism? The Arguments For and Against,* ed. Adrio König (Roodepoort, South Africa: CUM Books, 1984), pp. 125-38.

28. The Commission allows that candidates for "Affirmation of Baptismal Faith" might "use significant amounts of water with which to sign themselves (or even dip themselves)" but stresses that this affirmation is "a personal reminder of the baptism that has already taken place": see Commentary by the Liturgical Commission in *Christian Initiation,* pp. 349-50.

might be said by the administrant immersing the candidate? Some suggestions might be: "On the confession of your faith we immerse you to share with Christ in his death and his resurrection"; or "On the profession of your own faith, may you enter more deeply into the life of Christ and be filled with the Spirit." It is not possible, we see, to conceive a form of words for reaffirmation through immersion without some idea of the activity of the triune God in this event. It must be an effective sign of an ongoing "baptismal life" of dying and rising with Christ and being filled with the Spirit. Such a vision will, we have suggested, inform a commitment to mission and can be echoed in the concluding rite in which many from the congregation will "come down low" in order to be filled again with the Spirit. Perhaps the constant reference throughout the service to *all* the candidates as simply being "baptized," obscuring the distinction between those being baptized and those renewing baptismal vows, is an indication that some theological work still needs to be done.[29]

The second result of lack of attention to the activity of God is the absence of any *verbal* connection in this service between baptism and being received into the church. Of course, we have seen that the social aspect is very strongly present; the testimonies make clear that the journey of faith is made in the company, and with the encouragement of others, and particularly in the fellowship of the church. But what may be missing is the sense that believers do not just *join* a church, but have been gathered together by the action of God into the body of Christ, a summons to which they need to respond with obedience. Through baptism *God* gathers the church in all its diversity of membership. The church cannot exist as a particular social subset, say university students, though special provision may be made at times for particular groups. Unless Christian students are gathered into the church — with its whole range of age, ability and disability, ethnicity and intellectual variety — they will not continue in the church after university days are over. There is an excellent reminder of the life of the whole church in the service at St. Aldates in the video presentation of the "notices," showing many aspects of its mission outside the boundaries of student life. However, it is this summons into the church, and the activity of *God* in making a believer part of the whole body of Christ, that should be echoed in the baptismal liturgy.

At the end of the service the candidates were "welcomed back," but

---

29. After we shared the results of this observation with the leaders of the church, changes have in fact recently been made in the language of the rite.

there was no formal reception of the candidates into the church. It is a testimony to the warm fellowship of St. Aldates, an extraordinary example of a vibrant and contemporary church, that the candidates were in fact already "in the church," in the sense of being embraced and given support by many others. Clearly the rector felt this to be so. But opportunity could still have been taken to affirm and notice the action of God in forming Christ's people, so enabling disciples of Christ to enter more fully into the movement of God's own life and mission.

The service shows much evidence of participation in God, and as observers we have learned from the distinct form this takes in this particular congregation, whose worship is shaped by the creative merging of the several currents we have identified. In theological reflection on the service, we have been prompted to consider new "sacramental" forms of engaging the whole body in the movement of a God who is humbly giving God's own self in the world. In our turn, we have wanted to suggest ways in which this participation might be deepened in baptism, taking our cue from the rich potential that we experienced.

CHAPTER 4

Epiphanic Sacramentality: An Example of Practical Ecclesiology Revisioning Theological Understanding

Clare Watkins and Helen Cameron

With Deborah Bhatti, Catherine Duce, and James Sweeney

Commitment to interdisciplinary approaches characterizes practical theologies. In particular, those of us involved in various kinds of "practical ecclesiology" are familiar with the use of social-science methods as ways of better enabling our theological thinking about church by grounding it in real, lived experience and structures. We will be familiar, too, with the complexity of methodological and epistemological questions raised by such interdisciplinary work. What is, perhaps, less common is an appreciation of how the holding together of descriptive accounts of church practice with more traditional theological sources can both disclose something about the nature of the lived reality, and contribute to theological learning and pedagogy. The authors of this chapter, working with a distinctive methodology that they have developed over a number of years, believe that their practical-ecclesiological work with a number of church agencies demonstrates such disclosures. Reflection on these moments of

---

The multiple authorship of this chapter reflects the chapter's origin in team-based research through the project *Action Research — Church and Society.* The nature of this project — a collaboration between Heythrop College, University of London, and the Oxford Centre for Ecclesiology and Practical Theology (OxCEPT), Ripon College Cuddesdon — requires that recognition is given to all members of the team, as the significant insights and language of the research have been generated largely through shared conversation and mutual learning. For more about the ARCS project, see Helen Cameron, Deborah Bhatti, Catherine Duce, James Sweeney, and Clare Watkins, *Talking about God in Practice: Theological Action Research and Practical Theology* (London: SCM Press, 2010).

disclosure — or "epiphanies" — illustrates the value of such interdisciplinary method, not only for practice, but for theological vision more fundamentally.

To make this case, this chapter tells a "theological story" that involves us in accounts of *sacrament and sacramentality* from a variety of places in Christian thought and living. The focus on sacrament is not the only one we might have chosen. Other key themes emerging in our work have included authority and orders, community and communion, church and world; any of these — and others — might illustrate our claim just as well. Here, the systematic and practical themes of sacramental theology have been chosen as a particular and rich example. In the account that follows we first describe, using data gathered from particular church practices, incidents of what we have discerned as "sacramental moments" — or "sacramental epiphanies." This first stage involves a certain reflective reading of raw data witnessing to practices of faith as they are understood by the practitioners themselves, and is indebted to social-science methods and insights, especially from the field of action research. A second stage leads us to relate these embodied, theological voices to the more public voices of systematic theology regarding the sacramental, using distinctive methods developed by the authors' research work, *Action Research — Church and Society* (ARCS).

This bringing together of the theology expressed primarily through practice, and those theologies expressed primarily through words and concepts, discloses both various connections and disconnections — or fractures — between the embodied and the systematically articulated sacramental theologies. Such recognition of fractures leads us to reflect on their possible bases. We conclude by suggesting some possible remedies for the fractures, in the belief that the "fullness" of systematic theology requires a deep coherence between the ways in which faith is articulated, and the manner in which it is lived out, in the Christian community. It is significant that these conclusions draw us into an area that might be described as "formative theology." This term brings to the fore the various and complex ways in which Christians are "formed" in their faith, and suggests this locus as a place for particular attention. The question is: How might formation for "epiphanic sacramentality" be improved for both ministers/leaders and the Christian faithful as a whole?

A Preliminary Methodological Note — Theology in Four Voices

Insofar as this chapter offers a persuasive example of how interdisciplinary practical ecclesiological approaches can refresh theological thinking, it engages the reader in a number of case studies of particular faith practices. While a detailed account of each initiative studied, the particular methods used, and development of the authors' methodology cannot be given, a brief account of the main features of our approach will be helpful in grounding what follows.

The method employed in the ARCS research is described as "theological action research."[1] Theological action research is an approach to research that focuses on enabling practitioners to renew their practices or the meanings they attach to those practices. An outsider team (in this case the ARCS team) with expertise in research and relevant academic disciplines (sociological and theological) works in partnership with an insider team, who are close to the practice being studied. Together they design research questions, gather the data, and, through a process of structured dialogue, interpret the data with a view to changed practice or renewed theology. Theological action research starts with a *theological* question for research and then uses theological methods to interpret the data; it is thus characterized by being theological "all the way through," as well as by its being grounded in particular practices.

On one level this work can be seen as a fairly classic example of action research in getting insiders to compare what they said they did (their "espoused theology") with what they actually did (their "operant theology"). This critical bringing together of the espoused theology and operant theology was an important trigger for reflection, and led to discussions about whether what the group espoused needed to be moved closer to what it did, or whether what it did needed to be moved closer to what it espoused.[2]

What is particular to theological action research is the way that it

1. For a full account of theological action research, see Helen Cameron et al., *Talking about God in Practice: Theological Action Research and Practical Theology* (London: SCM Press, 2010).

2. Interestingly, we found that, despite the current vogue for vision and mission and values statements in the voluntary sector, a number of the organizations we worked with struggled to articulate their values, particularly in theological language. We now build the opportunity to do this into the setup phase of the research. See Helen Cameron et al., *Talking about God in Practice*, chapter 7.

deals explicitly with how the operant-espoused tension is to be understood, reflected on, and worked with. We do this by introducing two other terms — or "voices of theology" — alongside the operant and espoused "voices": the normative theological voice, referring to those texts and traditions of ecclesial teachings that a particular group may recognize as "authoritative" (e.g., Scripture, Church Councils, liturgies, etc.); and the formal theological voice, referring to the ideas and texts of "professional" theologians, of the theology of the academy, and its interdisciplinary partners.

As a team we use the term "the four voices of theology" to describe this commitment to an understanding of theology, which is found in the *conversation* and mutually critical engagement of these different theological authorities. This understanding of four voices is not to be understood as a separating out of "theologies," but rather a heuristic device for exploring what we believe is the to-be-hoped-for "full" picture of theology as something drawn from Christian practice, traditions, and intellectual life. So, "systematic theology" is not to be identified with one or other of these voices. Rather, the four-voices theology is — arguably — a particular (albeit limited) description of the dynamic traditions of systematic theology.

The naming of these "voices" ensures, first of all, that theological action research can remain true to its specifically theological commitment in understanding the practices themselves (operant theology) and the articulated theological intentions of practitioners (espoused theology) as an integral part of the whole theological "conversation." In addition, the four-voices framework enables connections to be made across the key theological areas represented, in ways that may be mutually informative and shaping. This interpretative device also, of course, discloses where communication and connection have failed in some way.

The present chapter can be read as a demonstration of how — in the particular systematic area of sacramental theology — the four-voices approach to theological action research can enable an improved contribution to the debate from the theological authority that is Christian practice.

Epiphanic Sacramentality: The Data

The interpretative work of theological action research is done by conversation both within insider and outsider teams and between them, as they reflect on data describing the practices being researched. It proceeds by a number of small epiphanies when something is seen differently because of the different perspectives around the table or there is a moment of shared insight that was not there at the start of the meeting. Judith Thompson picks up this idea as part of the pastoral cycle and uses Andrew Todd's phrase of "the kairos moment," a moment when the tradition and reflection on practice trigger an insight that in turn will prompt fresh thinking or action.[3] These kairos moments, or small epiphanies, are made possible not only by the data and references to the tradition in front of the meeting, but also by the formation — spiritual, pastoral, and academic — that team members bring to the meeting.

In describing the data upon which we wish to reflect in this chapter, one route would be to flatten them into the expected social-science account, logically ordered and abstracted from the messiness of the research process. This would subvert the purposes of this chapter, which are concerned with the authentic, often incremental and "messy" ways in which moments of epiphany occur in real case studies of practice. Instead, this section attempts to describe how this particular segment of data has come to our attention as theologically significant for what it says about sacrament and sacramentality. In principle, it is the reflective journey through the data that will disclose the theological reality we have named "epiphanic sacramentality," and for this reason it is not appropriate to our understanding to define it at this early stage. What can, perhaps, be said is that the particular data described here triggered, in various ways and various research constituencies, "epiphanies" of the kind just described, which clustered around theological themes of sacrament and sacramentality. We believe that, reading these data through the conversational methods demanded by the four-voices approach, fresh insights can be made for a systematic theological approach to sacrament, and its communication and effectiveness in the life of the church.

Data 1: Housing Justice (Cycle 1)

Housing Justice is a national ecumenical faith-based agency offering support to Christian groups and charities addressing housing issues and lobbying for improvements in public policy. One of the initiatives it supports is the Winter Night Shelter organization run by groups of churches in some London Boroughs. Winter Night Shelters usually comprise seven churches that are able to allow rough sleepers to sleep in a makeshift dor-

3. Judith Thompson, *Theological Reflection* (London: SCM Press, 2008), chapter 5.

mitory in their church premises for one night a week in the months of January to March.

Housing Justice and the coordinator of one Winter Night Shelter wanted to conduct research into the motivations of guests and volunteers associated with the Night Shelter. They were in search of an answer to the question that so many faith-based agencies ask: What difference does the "faith" element make to our service provision? In collaboration with the ARCS team it was agreed that the ARCS fieldworker would gather data through a focus group with guests and a focus group with volunteers, in one Anglican and one Roman Catholic church taking part in the shelter, and interview the two parish priests. The findings were unexpected to both the insider team and the ARCS team.

First, it was generally the case that the guests at the night shelters were clear that they were sleeping on church premises and that they valued the holistic care provided, which they compared favorably with other agencies. A number of guests used explicitly christological language to describe their encounter with the church:

> Tell you what, it's like God has let you into his house. If you want to look at it in a deep way it's like God has said come into my house and get out of the cold. That's if you want to look at it in a deep spiritual way.
>
> Voice 5

> I am finding it interesting that despite the difference of the churches here — being it a this or a that church — actually they're coming together as a Body, as it should be, in the Body of Christ and actually working together and establishing some sort of unity and strength in unity together to help the outside. I'm finding it really interesting that they are working together instead of going against each other.
>
> Voice 2

A second observation makes a striking counterpoint to this: volunteers at the night shelters, most but not all of whom were church members, were reluctant to connect their motivation to volunteer with their faith. They felt that they were no better than other people and that they were making a human response to human need. Volunteers showed a marked reluctance to use explicitly faith language to describe what they did.

One quotation from a volunteer seemed to leap off the page as an exception:

Occasionally Louis will ring me up to say can you come down here early because we're short of numbers. I will just miss Mass, or come out of Mass early. I could stand there through the Mass and I enjoy Mass and I'm there for different reasons and values, but I'd much sooner do this if I had the choice between the two — in terms of the importance. It's all very well saying you love God, but if you've sat upstairs knowing that down below they are rushed off their feet in the kitchen that would just be ridiculous.

Richard, Winter Night Shelter Volunteer

The striking nature of this volunteer's contribution led to intense conversation in the ARCS group, sparking certain moments of disclosure. It was energetically debated whether or not this volunteer had made the connection between the sacrament of the Mass and the sacramentality of the meal being prepared for the homeless. Opinions diverged in revealing ways on the theological significance of this quotation: Helen, a Salvationist, immediately leapt to the conclusion that the quotation was an epiphany of a realized eschatology when, in the enactment of the kingdom on earth as it is in heaven, the need for the temple falls away; Clare, a Roman Catholic, used an analogical approach and saw the grace of the Eucharist overflowing into the grace of the meal being prepared downstairs and the grace of the social action informing the experience of sacramental grace in the Eucharist.

In feedback to the Housing Justice insider team, we found that they were equally perplexed by the inability of the volunteers to make the connection between their eucharistic celebrations and the meals they were preparing for the homeless guests. It was agreed that a second cycle of research would consist of focus groups of volunteers who would be given anonymized quotes from guests to reflect upon. Surely seeing the language of the guests would give them permission to reflect more theologically on the influence of their faith on their volunteering. However, we would have to wait for our answer, as the Night Shelters would not recommence for another nine months.

Data 2: St. Mary's Battersea and the Alpha Course

The ARCS team approached St. Mary's Battersea as a church that advertised on its website that it ran the Alpha course regularly. As a research project interested in the evangelization work of London churches, we were interested in how Christian inquiry courses were used, and work had already been done with CaFE (Catholic Faith Exploration), a provider of Roman Catholic inquiry and adult formation courses. For their part, St. Mary's responded to our overture because they were interested in asking what led someone from being a new attender to a more committed member of the church. They had a high turnover in membership (about 25 percent every four years), as couples moved out of central London once children were born, and those in employment had highly mobile jobs. Although identifying themselves as an inclusive church of the liberal Catholic tradition, they had found the Alpha course a useful way of incorporating new attenders into the life of the church. Interviews were done by the ARCS fieldworker with a mix of attenders and leaders of the Alpha course. The data evoked a range of reflections and helped the church reconceptualize its problem of commitment.

> When I first started coming to St. Mary's I was still working then. I came to recharge my batteries, and I tended to come to the 8 a.m. where it was quiet and there were no children, and I didn't necessarily have to talk to anyone if I didn't want to, so it was an oasis! But as the years have gone on, you realize that it is not all about pleasing yourself and that it's also about being part of the body of Christ so that you need to meet and make contact with and understand and be there for other people, not just for yourself, however pleasant it is. So that's the difference.
>
> Alpha Participant

In the course of an ARCS team reflection on the data, we noticed that there was very little reference to Jesus or Christ in the data, and noted this with surprise given our knowledge of the content of the Alpha course. Going back to the data we noted a number of relevant concerns: about assuming a Christian identity in central London; about offending people of other faiths; about attracting an aggressive secularity from work colleagues; and about appearing to be the "wrong sort" of Christian, who would aggressively proselytize rather than be spiritual. It was realized that language about Christ touched on all these sensitivities. Interestingly, the insider team at St. Mary's had not themselves picked up on this apparent christological lack. When it was raised with them through the sharing of the reflections from ARCS, a moment of silence was quickly broken by the comment that, "Well, I suppose we're not a very 'Jesus' parish" — and then a spontaneous laughter, as people recognized something significant here, an epiphanic moment. Going forward, the place of the proclamation of Jesus Christ became an important consideration for the parish team, as they worked to look again at the way in which it taught about Christ.

Reflecting on the St. Mary's data again for this chapter we were struck again at the emphasis in this "not a very 'Jesus' parish" on weekly attendance at the Eucharist. A difficult but significant question arises here as to how this liturgical-sacramental emphasis connects (or fails to connect) with reluctance to talk about Christ.

Data 3: Diocese of Westminster Justice and Peace Commission and Fair Trade

Most Roman Catholic dioceses have a Justice and Peace Commission that supports parish Justice and Peace groups and takes initiatives to promote relevant activities at parish level. The Diocese of Westminster Justice and Peace Commission wanted to investigate how parishes understood its support of Fair Trade. Interviews were undertaken in parishes as the basis for reflection. From these it was clear that those active in promoting the Fair Trade goods had mostly understood the message of justice they conveyed. For some parishioners, however, the purchase of the goods was more simply seen as philanthropic, and on a par with donations to aid agencies. The frustration for those actively involved in Fair Trade lay with the lack of connection that seemed apparent between *justice* and faith, among church people for whom faith and charity were self-evidently (if unreflectively) linked. The question then arises as to how such connection might be understood, and better made.

Reflecting on these data, we were struck by the parallel of the altar at the front of the church with the eucharistic meal, and the table at the back of the church with the Fair Trade food. The sheer geography of this underlined, for us as "theologically trained" observers, the issue of connecting the Eucharist as an enactment of the kingdom of justice and peace, and the opportunity to buy Fair Trade goods. Making this connection was also an instinct evident among the Fair Trade workers themselves, albeit one struggling for clear articulation:

> I think that if we were bringing [Fair Trade] up more often in the liturgy, if it was something they were hearing on a more regular basis be-

cause you know, Mass is where you are fed your things to think about in terms of your faith. So I think that, but also I think there is a thing about people's . . . living your life, being a witness, trying to be an example to others.

Parish Fair Trade Coordinator

Data 4: Housing Justice (Cycle 2)

We can now return to the questions raised by our first set of data from Housing Justice (Data 1 above). Having been surprised by the theological explicitness of the guests' language, in contrast to the volunteers' reticence about faith, we now found ourselves surprised again. For, when the connection between the hospitality of the Eucharist and the hospitality to the homeless guests was pointed out to volunteers, while there were points of recognition, there was a clear resistance to embracing this interpretation.

Catholic Church

Cath: A reenactment of the Last Supper, do you make that kind of connection?

John: Sorry, I totally missed that point!! (a lot of laughter)

Priest: Let us break bread together, you know, that's something of it, that we break bread, that I am breaking my bread. People are bringing food. . . .

Jean: I don't make that connection.

Jade: I don't think about it. I mean yes, it's through my church but I don't automatically link it with the Eucharist.

Jean: You're not doing it because of the church; you're doing it because you want to do it? *(Several agree.)*

Anglican Church

Sally: Do you make any connections between communion and volunteering at the shelter?

Jan: Sharing the meal.

Liberty: Oh yes!

Jan: Sharing the meals, sitting down, and everyone is kind of equal together. Everyone sat together in the evenings.

Theresa: The fellowship aspect. Yes.

Lee: I was about to say that communion in church is seen as rather detached from what it was based on anyway. I mean you could say something like the Last Supper is much more of a meal that happens downstairs whereas communion always seems rather artificial and rather detached from that, because of the process it goes through; it doesn't feel like a meal and sitting down and being in community together. Maybe that's why there's not such an obvious connection in our minds.

What seems clear is that, even when the connection between Eucharist and feeding the homeless is made and understood, it fails to be an active or appropriated interpretation for the volunteers. The ritualized, "sacral" expression of meal in the Eucharist seems hard to relate to the real, down-to-earth activity of the shelters; the experiences are too different. It may be significant that, in reflecting upon this outcome in the joint meeting with the Housing Justice team, one person pointed out that for Roman Catholics the Eucharist is special, "sacred," and to associate it with something as mundane as preparing food for homeless people could be seen as disrespectful.

Moments of Disclosure: Reading the Data through the Four Voices

The data described already offer some interesting insights into practices and their particular relation to — or disconnect from — sacramental understanding and practice; a productive work of action research could be carried out simply through practitioner reflections on the questions that have already been identified. However, the particular contribution of *theological* action research is to provide a framework for reflection that enables reflectors to engage not only with practice and its immediate contextual interpretation, but also with normative and formal voices of theology, which speak into the practices described. This is where the four voices of theology, set out earlier, come into play.

In this section we will begin to make some observations about how the four voices of theology enable a particular reading of sacramental theology through the data described in section two. We will be concerned with identifying both connection and tensions between different voices, and — where necessary — demonstrating where apparent fractures or breakdowns in communication between the different aspects of theology have occurred.

Some Observations from the Operant Theology of Sacrament

What the data described represent — in different contexts — are a number of ways in which practices of Christians embody some sense of the "presence" of Christ in the ordinary; in a number of cases this presence is associated with food, meals, and fellowship in ways that resonate strongly with the liturgical practices of sacrament (Eucharist) in which all these church groups are formed in some way. The practices of outreach sit alongside eucharistic worship in ways that highlight both the connection and *lack* of connection between these two aspects of church life.

So, the table spread with Fair Trade food, speaking of the call to solidarity with the poor and justice in the ways we live, shares the same space as the table of Eucharist — the table of thanksgiving, of Christ's sacrifice, and of foot washing and service. Similarly, the tables spread for those in most need, through homelessness and poverty, are architecturally alongside the altar, where Christians are fed by the abiding presence and love of God in Jesus, in a sacramental-liturgical way. And the practices of welcome and outreach are carried out by a people held together by their weekly celebration of Eucharist, where Jesus, who ate with sinners, welcomes everyone. In all these examples our routine naming of sacrament — which is primarily liturgical in the parish setting — comes up against what can be recognized as real lived practices of sacrament outside, but alongside, the liturgical.

Some Observations from the Espoused Theologies of Sacrament

Typically, in the groups we have worked with, the espoused sacramental theology will be relatively weak, perhaps reflecting these groups' self-conscious orientation toward outreach and social justice. This observation is especially interesting when we remember that we are working with highly "liturgical" traditions, in which the practice of regular eucharistic celebration is an assumed part of Christian living. Still, when the mission statements and overt understanding of these groups is examined, the espoused theologies do not seem to require an especially sacramental vision. The challenge then becomes the tension that exists between this apparently a-sacramental espoused theology and the operant theologies that, in contrast, suggest powerful connections between social and evangelizing mission and the sacramental life.

The recognition of such a tension is the beginning of the reflections into which both (insider) practitioners and (outsider) ARCS teams are called by the research. What cannot be anticipated is how such a disclosure of tension might be received. So, the sacramental epiphany in the first phase of Housing Justice, while recognized by both the ARCS team and the Housing Justice leaders, was not appropriated by the body of practitioners themselves. The connection between Eucharist and justice practices that seem to be called for was felt unnecessary — even unhelpful — for the work. For all that, in terms of the dynamics of systematic theology, the embodied operant sacramental theology, in tension with the espoused theology, which resists such sacramental naming, still has an important part to play in the complex reading of sacramentality in today's church. In particular, it raises the question as to why so many Christians *resist* a connection between their works of care and their lives of worship and sacrament.

Some Observations from Normative Theologies of Sacrament

When speaking of "normative" theology in these contexts, the first thing to recognize is the ways in which this might be variously understood among practitioners. In particular, the tendency is for Roman Catholic groups — especially those working under "official" auspices of, say, a diocese (as in the case of the Justice and Peace Commission) — to have a stronger sense of the normative role of certain theological sources than Anglican groups. For sure, the Lambeth-Chicago quadrilateral does clearly name normative sources for Anglican understanding — Scripture, tradition, reason, and experience — but the possible variety of emphases and interrelatedness of these sources open up a wide spectrum of interpretation and theological culture at the level of parish community. In turn, this variety of ecclesial culture with regard to what is normative may make the very discussion of "normative theology" uncomfortable for many Anglicans. In a parish such as St. Mary's, Battersea, with so strong an emphasis on inclusivity and liberal outlook, these discomforts may be especially keenly felt.

However, even given the difficulties of speaking "evenly" about normative theological voices across the practices, a number of helpful observations may be made.

First, we need to recognize the place occupied by liturgical practices of Eucharist as a source of normative theology in all our practitioner groups. Indeed, there is, perhaps, no stronger "ordinary" normative theological expression than the regular and commonly shared experience of Eucharist. Such a regular participation in normative theology and its texts is a remarkable phenomenon; but what is perhaps most striking in the data is the way in which this very present, well-known normative voice *fails* to engage thoroughly with the embodied eucharistic practices that reflection identified. We have here a first question about the apparent breakdown of communication between the normative and operant-espoused voices: *What might be preventing a more fruitful conversation between the normative theology of liturgical practice and the embodied sacramental theologies of outreach practices?*

This question is particularly puzzling when we become aware of the ways in which the normative theology of the Catholic Church, as expressed in magisterial teaching, speaks quite clearly of the embodiment of sacramental understanding in nonliturgical practices. In Benedict XVI's recent Apostolic Exhortation, the practice of "eucharistic living" after the liturgical celebration is given a section to itself, as it is made clear that

> Christians, in all their actions, are called to offer true worship to God. Here the intrinsically eucharistic nature of Christian life begins to take shape. The Eucharist, since it embraces the concrete, everyday existence of the believer, makes possible, day by day, the progressive transfiguration of all those called by grace to reflect the image of the Son of God (cf. Rom. 8:29ff.). There is nothing authentically human — our thoughts and affections, our words and deeds — that does not find in the sacrament of the Eucharist the form it needs to be lived to the full . . .[4]

Nor is this account strange to Catholic thinking. It can also be recognized in the Second Vatican Council's understanding of the priestly office of the baptized,[5] and in certain passages of John Paul II's last encyclical, *Ecclesia de Eucharistia*.[6]

For all Christians, there is a certain biblical understanding of sacrament that links sacrament and ethic. So, in 1 Corinthians 10–11 Paul's account of the institution of the Eucharist is set in the context of an ethical

---

4. Benedict XVI, Apostolic Exhortation, *Sacramentum Caritatis* (2007), n. 71.

5. So see the Second Vatican Council's Dogmatic Constitution on the Church, *Lumen Gentium*, n. 34, and the Constitution on the Sacred Liturgy, *Sacrosanctum Concilium*, nn. 9–10.

6. See John Paul II's encyclical *Ecclesia de Eucharistia* (2003), n. 22, for example.

exhortation: the practice of Eucharist tells the Christians of Corinth how they are to relate to one another. We might also reflect on the parallel of the institution of the Eucharist in the synoptic Gospels with the foot washing of John's Gospel, and the ways in which other texts remind us of the ethical consequences of baptism in terms of teaching, obedience, equality, and unity.[7]

What is remarkable in these examples is the extent to which, on an "official" normative level, the realities of "epiphanic sacramentality" are recognized and named from a place that is, empirically at least, apart from these practices. A living connection between the normative and the operant is revealed, in a perhaps surprising (though ecclesiologically affirming?) way; yet the evidence is that Christian practitioners either do not know of, or misunderstand, this normative voice of their own tradition. For example, the participant's observation concerning the "sacredness" of the Eucharist, which separates it from the "ordinary" activities of charity, is clearly at odds with these normative theologies of sacrament and ethic. The data witness to the reality that this connection is missed by those "on the ground." And so a second question concerning the lack of conversation between the voices arises: *What are the key mechanisms by which the normative voices of Scripture and church teaching are heard at the level of Christian practice; and what is impeding this conversation taking place more fruitfully?*

Some Observations from Formal Theologies of Sacrament

We can observe, across the ARCS research, that it is the formal voice of theology that is least well engaged with in the practices we have worked with; there may even be a degree of resistance from practitioners concerning this form of theological articulation. This resistance can be understood in terms of the "professionalization" of theology through its formal development, and the sense therefore, that it is "not for the likes of us." This is part of the tragedy of contemporary Christian theology to which practical theologies are especially concerned to respond. For ARCS there is a need to push beyond this basic observation of difficulty, and inquire more specifically into the possibilities for a systematic theology in which practice has its place.

There is a particular place in our work where the formal voice does

---

7. For example, Matthew 28:18-20; 1 Corinthians 1; Galatians 3:25-28; Ephesians 4:4-6.

make itself inevitably heard. What enabled the ARCS team to make the connections between practice and sacrament — what made the moment of sacramental epiphany possible — was the voice of "formal theology," insofar as it is a part of the skills base present in the ARCS team personnel. We mention this here as it raises the important question of the "role of the expert" in the processes of practical and reflective theology. We believe our processes of theological action research, built around conversation and shared reflection, allow for the outsider group to bring *different* knowledge, on an equal rather than expert basis. An expertise in formal theology is clearly necessary for the effectiveness of the reflections across the four voices; but it is also, crucially, an expertise placed at service to the conversation rather than one that expects a deferral to the expert.

What the formal theological training of ARCS team members has been able to bring to the reading of these practices is an awareness of a surprising set of connections between the "epiphanic sacramentality" disclosed in the reflection on practice, and certain aspects of contemporary formal theology. In fact, there is a certain small and rather disparate body of literature in sacramental theology that specifically argues that liturgical sacramental celebration is "completed" or fulfilled in Christian practices of justice, charity, and outreach; and that the celebration of Eucharist gathers up into that sacrament of the church the "worldly sacramental" lived eucharistic graces of ordinary Christian living. For example, Luis Segundo, as a liberation theologian, is critical of a sacramental approach characterized by "our pagan insistence on the altar";[8] and others, from the perspective of moral theology, argue with him for a greater sense of connection between Eucharist and justice practices.[9]

This literature is predominantly Catholic; but we can see a similar thread in Anglican thinking.[10] These movements in sacramental theology in the West may also be recognized as influenced by certain themes of East-

8. Juan Luis Segundo, *Theology for Artisans of a New Humanity (vol. 4): The Sacraments Today* (Maryknoll, NY: Orbis, 1973), p. 8. See, in similar vein, Tissa Balasuriya, *The Eucharist and Human Liberation* (London: SCM, 1979).

9. See Enda McDonagh, "Fruit of the Earth — Work of Human Hands," in *The Candles Are Still Burning: Directions in Sacrament and Spirituality,* ed. Mary Grey (London: Geoffrey Chapman, 1995), pp. 22-31; and Bernard Häring, *The Sacraments in a Secular Age: A Vision in Depth on Sacramentality and Its Impact on Moral Life* (Slough, UK: St. Paul Publications, 1976).

10. For example, John Macquarrie, *A Guide to the Sacraments* (London: SCM, 1997). We would also mention the influential work of the Methodist scholar James F. White, *Sacraments as God's Self Giving* (Nashville: Abingdon, 1983).

ern theology, most notably the idea of "the liturgy after the liturgy." Of this Anastasios Yannoulatos writes: "Each of the faithful is called upon to continue a personal liturgy on the secret altar of his own heart, to realize a living proclamation of the good news 'for the sake of the kingdom.' Without this continuation the liturgy remains incomplete."[11] The ecumenically common drives to mission, and to engagement with cultural concerns such as environmental and global political issues, have also added to this sense of an urgency to understand sacramental practice beyond the liturgical.[12]

This all-too-brief account of "embodied sacramentality" in formal theology highlights not only a fascinating resonance between contemporary theology and contemporary practice; it also raises the question as to why, given this resonance, there is so little explicit engagement between these voices. *Why is it that the common concerns of the formal and the operant nonetheless fail to connect in mutually informative and life-giving ways?*

Conclusion: The Four Voices in Systematic Theology — Responding to Fractures in the Conversation

The theological reading of our data for "epiphanic sacramentality" has enabled us to identify both a harmony of theological voices and a set of failures of mutual engagement between the voices. Such a picture describes the fragmented nature of systematic theology for and in the church of our own time. As this chapter's explorations draw to a close, we can offer a tentative preliminary thesis that goes something like this:

> Exploration of the ways in which sacramental theology is both embodied and articulated in a "full" systematics of word and practice suggests that — while there is an emerging theme across the voices concerning epiphanic sacramentality, or the disclosure of sacrament in the ordinary — this resonance is barely recognized. The authors of this chapter argue that, for the proper fullness of systematic thinking, these voices need to be in explicit and attentive conversation with one another, and so attention must be given to the questions of what enables and disables such conversation.

11. Cited by Ion Bria, *The Liturgy after the Liturgy* (Geneva: WCC Publications, 1996), p. 20.

12. An outstanding example of this would be William T. Cavanaugh, *Torture and Eucharist: Theology, Politics and the Body of Christ* (Oxford: Blackwell, 1998).

The particularity and specificity of our work, and its particular attention to practice, has enabled us to identify a number of questions relating to these fractures in the conversation of systematic theology. To recap:

1. *What might be preventing a more fruitful conversation between the normative theology of liturgical practice and the embodied sacramental theologies of outreach practices?*
2. *What are the key mechanisms by which the normative voices of Scripture and church teaching are heard at the level of Christian practice; and what is impeding this conversation from taking place more fruitfully?*
3. *Why is it that the common concerns of the formal and the operant nonetheless fail to connect in mutually informative and life-giving ways?*

In our discussions of these three questions, three areas for further examination have come to light: the ritualization of the normative in liturgy and its effects; the place of "formative theology" in enabling or disabling epiphanic sacramentality; and the overall contribution of these insights of theological action research for systematic theological approaches to sacramental theology. We can set them out as questions for discussion thus:

1. How does the (normative) ritualization of the sacramental in Roman Catholic and Anglican traditions affect "the liturgy after the liturgy," and so the possibilities for "epiphanic sacramentality"?
2. What does this discussion suggest for the practices of "formative theology" — the theological formation and training of both ministers and laity? How might such formative theology enable (or not) an epiphanic sacramental approach?
3. What difference might the insights of this exploration make to the practice of systematic theology, especially in the areas of sacramental theology and liturgical theology?

This chapter has demonstrated two things. The first is the fruitfulness of exploring a systematic theological term — in this case, sacrament — through the practical theological method of theological action research. The fruitfulness of such an approach lies chiefly in its ability to hold together a variety of different "voices," aware of their different respective authorities and their ecclesiological coherence, and so offer a presentation of systematic theology as a conversational reality. It is an approach that has enabled us in particular, to speak of sacramental theology in terms of "epiphanic sacramentality" — a theology of sacrament that, drawing on practice in a particular way, broadens and deepens the sacramental beyond the liturgical. This theological approach has enabled a clearer identification of one aspect of normative and formal theologies that seems especially resonant with practice.

This practical-systematic theology of sacrament has also disclosed a second thing: the existence of some significant failures within this conversational reality that diminish both practical and formal/normative voices of theology, and so diminish the possibilities of a systematic theological account of sacrament. In our own tentative reflections we have suggested that the areas of formation (ministerial and lay), and of liturgical practice, present themselves as places for renewal for the improvement of this conversation. There is, here, a call to practitioners and theologians to open up new ways of dialogue so as to enable the many-voiced theological conversation that is necessary to a "full" and effective theological endeavor.

PART THREE

On Congregations and Society

Understanding Religion Takes Practice: Anti-Urban Bias, Geographical Habits, and Theological Influences

Mark T. Mulder and James K. A. Smith

Introduction: The Devil in the City?

Having emerged from its assumed rural homeland, evangelicalism has not exactly made its way to the city. Rather, it is often seen as a quintessentially suburban phenomenon (Green and Greenberg 2004; Mulder and Smith 2009). We see this impression in influential journalistic accounts of conservative Protestants. For instance, Jeff Sharlet, based on discussions with congregants from New Life Church on the northern edge of Colorado Springs, noted a pattern regarding evangelical perceptions of the city. According to these suburban parishioners,

> [c]ities are especially dangerous. It is not so much the large populations, with their uneasy mix of sinner and saved, that make Christian conservatives leery of urban areas. Even downtown Colorado Springs, presumably as godly as any big town in America, struck the New Lifers as unclean. Whenever I asked where to eat, they would warn me away from downtown's neat little grid of cafés and ethnic joints. Stick to Academy, they'd tell me, referring to the vein of superstores and prepackaged eateries that bypasses the city. (Sharlet 2005, 49)

If this vignette is at all representative, evangelicals exhibit a particular (and particularly intense) version of a uniquely American phenomenon: an anti-urban bias that fosters fear of the city and flight to suburban settlement.

This perceived "suburban-ness" of evangelicals raises a number of questions that require not only a sociological but also a theological approach. First, is this common picture warranted? Can the perception be solidified with social-scientific research? Second, if we can confirm a suburban "center of gravity" for evangelicalism, can we discern the causes of such, or at least discern key factors that might account for such a correlation?[1] Our goal in this chapter is to use this particular case study as a catalyst for articulating a necessary partnership between theology and sociology, working in tandem to understand the nature of faithful practice.

Disciplining Ecclesiology, Thickening Sociology: Methodological Orientation

Our research investigates a complex, layered social phenomenon: evangelicalism's relationship to the city. On a more fine-grained level, we are specifically interested in evangelical perceptions of the urban core of metropolitan areas and their relationship to suburban and exurban social arrangements — with background concern about the social, political, and environmental impact of suburban expansion (Jackson 1985). Dealing with such social complexity requires an equally complex methodological approach. In particular, we are convinced that this requires the nuances of a sociologically disciplined theology and a theologically informed sociology. We would outline three components of this methodological orientation — three ways in which theology needs sociology and sociology needs theology.

Sociology, Normativity, and Theology

Discerning religious influences on anti-urban bias and geographical habits is an example of just the sort of complex phenomenon that eludes explanation by reductionistic approaches. Such reductionistic models have massive blind spots that will not permit sociological observation to *see* cultural phenomena that refuse to squeeze through this narrow gate.[2] Thus,

1. There is a third, more normative, line of research that we cannot pursue in this chapter: How might evangelicals think critically about both their anti-urban bias and their suburban location? Might these raise questions of *justice*? Could it be that the geographical habits of evangelicals actually run counter to some of their own theological intuitions?

2. This would be an instance of what Thomas Kuhn would describe as a "paradigm

contesting reductionisms of various stripes, Christian Smith is especially critical of methodologies that reduce humans to merely economic or biological animals; in contrast, he argues that sociologies that attend to the cultural aspects of human society yield more fruitful, persuasive accounts of complex social phenomena. In particular, Smith argues for the importance of seeing human beings as also moral, believing, storytelling animals.[3] Such a nonreductionistic approach — working with "thicker" assumptions about human persons and communities — provides a wider theoretical gate that is able to account for the complexity of social phenomena.[4]

Our approach aims to work with a "thicker" account of human persons and communities in order to prime observation that is open and able to see other cultural influences at work. The goal is a social science that is more attentive to the nitty-gritty particularity of cultural webs of meaning and semiotic systems (of which particular theologies and ecclesiologies are instances). This is not a matter of theology loading the dice, or prescribing ahead of time what can be seen. In other words, this is not a sly way of letting theology into the conversation only to shut it down. Instead, the goal is to draw on the particularities of theology — including dogmatic, confessional theology — in order to appreciate the nuances and fine-grained detail of particular religious communities and traditions. Theology can be

---

effect." Sharp (2007), C. Smith (2003), and others are out to contest the governing paradigms that constitute "normal science" (and hence "orthodoxy") in the social sciences.

3. While we cannot fully address concerns here, it should be noted that Smith's epistemological claims here are nuanced. He is not advocating a metaphysical essentialism that he thinks is yielded by "pure" reason. That is, the warrant for these richer models of the human person (as a moral, believing animal) cannot be "proven" by appeal to transcendent rational criteria. Rather, akin to Milbank, Smith would argue that the proof is in the pudding; that is, the proof that such non-reductionistic models are "better" for explaining social phenomena is that they do a better job of giving an account of the "given" social realities that we bump up against or that push back on our accounts. We might describe this as Smith's nonfoundationalist essentialism. For more on this, see C. Smith 2003, 87-91.

4. Smith's methodological manifesto should also come as a challenge to much work in "congregational studies," which often works with a reductionistic model of congregations and denominations that reduces the church to just one more "organization" and fails to be attentive to the particularities of *ecclesiology*. Smith's core argument is that the "scientific" study of religion does not require reducing the religious to the non-religious. Or positively, the scientific study of religion *requires* the adoption of non-reductionistic models of the human person and religious belief. So also, sociological investigation of the church *needs* to be informed by ecclesiology. For relevant discussion, see Kenneson 1999, 60; Mulder and Smith 2010.

seen as the explication of the meaning-systems that constitute the "culture" of religious traditions and practices. In this mode, theology functions *as* cultural theory, and theologians are resourced as attentive phenomenologists of the habits, practices, and beliefs of religious communities (J. K. A. Smith 1999, 25-28).

Our methodological approach is also grounded in our conviction that all social science is ineluctably informed by pretheoretical, extrascientific commitments that are ultimately theological in nature. In short, we reject the notion of a "secular" social science (cf. Milbank 1990; J. K. A. Smith 2004). But contrary to a common misunderstanding, the rejection of "secular" social science is not a rejection of social science *qua* science. Rather, it simply contests the claim that social-scientific observation is religiously neutral and not governed by extrascientific assumptions. The implication is not to thereby rule out any sociology that is "not Christian"; instead, the point is to level the playing field by pressing the sciences to own up to this and thereby engender a genuinely *pluralist* field.

In this sense, Christian Smith's project is akin to Milbank's: Smith wants to push social scientists (and sociologists in particular) to own up to the fact that their work is driven by particular (nonscientific) models and assumptions about human persons and human societies. Because these models and assumptions are so widely accepted (they constitute what Kuhn would call "orthodoxy" or "normal science"), many social scientists fall into the trap of just thinking "that's the way things are." In this context or environment, Smith wants to do three things:

1. Point out the models that constitute the regnant paradigms in the human sciences and show them to be "paradigms" (i.e., pre- and extrascientific constellations of assumptions);
2. Subject these models to critique for being too reductionistic and thus not able to do justice to the phenomena that present themselves; and
3. Show that a "thicker" (nonreductionist) understanding of human persons as "moral, believing animals" does a better job of accounting[5] for the social phenomena that give themselves.

5. That is, Smith is not out to "prove" that the model of persons as moral, believing animals is true by some kind of independent demonstration; rather (akin to Milbank), he wants to show that this model shows itself to be true because it can do a better job of accounting for the social phenomena that give themselves (i.e., that "push back" on us). To use Milbank's term, Smith's project is one of out-narrating, not demonstrating.

These claims relate not only to social theory, but also observation. All observation — all "seeing" — is also shaped and governed by pretheoretical and extrascientific assumptions. In particular, our observation is driven by assumptions about the nature of human persons and human community. Embedded in every instrument and implicit in every questionnaire is a set of *norms,* an implicit set of assumptions about what human beings are (and *ought* to be) and what community is (and *should* look like). The interests, questions, and observations of social scientists cannot help but be informed by implicit visions of "the good life" — understandings of human flourishing. Once again, this is not a situation to be lamented (in which case we would be positivists in despair), but rather a situation to which the social sciences need to "own up" by putting their assumptions on the table and making them available for critique. "Interested" observation is not invalid; rather, the claim is that all observation has "interests," and pre-observational assumptions about what's at stake.[6]

Once this situation is appreciated, then the playing field is leveled and we should then be free to work from specifically Christian theoretical assumptions — provided we follow the same rules, namely, that we put these on the table and make them available for critique. Thus our project tries to undertake a mode of sociological research that is unapologetically informed by a distinctly Christian theory of urban social relations — but also seeks to be accountable to empirical realities. One of our goals in this project is to exhibit a kind of sociological research that avoids both theory-driven blindness to empirical data as well as a naïve positivism about empirical description. All empirical observation, we would argue, is filtered through a constellation of assumptions and commitments. At the same time, theory must be field-tested and verified in the arena of empirical experience. To paraphrase Kant, theory without observation is empty; observation without theory is blind.

All sociological research, then, is theory-driven and all sociological observation is informed by theoretical commitments that are themselves informed by extrascientific, ultimately religious commitments. It is precisely recognition of this situation that opens the space for the "admittance," as it were, of sociological research oriented by theory that is distinctly Christian. We believe that social-science research that is distinctly Christian must work from robust theological assumptions about what it means to be human, the shape of human community, the breakdown of

6. This is not just some "postmodern" claim. It is as old as Weber.

relationships, and the hope for new social configurations. However, Christian sociological theory that remains *a priori* speculation is not properly sociological. It must be supplemented and opened to confirmation (or *dis*confirmation) in the arena of experience through empirical observation. Our research initiative on urban sociality seeks to enact this vision of sociological research.

Attention to Lived Theology and Liturgical Habits

Our project is concerned with the "geographical habits" of evangelicals — the rhythms and patterns of their practices with respect to *place*. More specifically, we are interested in considering the relation between geographical habits, religious practices, and theological traditions. What sorts of geographical habits do evangelicals exhibit? Have these changed over time, or not? Is it the case that they gravitate toward the suburbs? If so, why? Are some of the distinctives of evangelical faith and practice relevant factors with respect to these habits?[7] How do these differ from other religious traditions? Answering these sorts of questions requires careful attunement to the nuances and particularities of evangelical spirituality, theology, and practice. And *that* requires a sociology that is informed by the insights of theology.

But not just any theology either. Questions about religion and place have not often been asked in existing social-scientific analyses of evangelicals; we suggest this stems from the fact that sociology of religion over the past decade has been largely interested in politics, "values," and moral patterns. And this interest itself stems from a basic methodological assumption: that human persons are basically "thinking things," or at best "believing things," where "believing" is reduced to propositional content. This is then easily wed to theological paradigms that also tend to overemphasize the cognitive and propositional (doctrines, ideas, values) rather than embodiment and practice. Thus in the very shape of its instruments, sociology of religion operates with a "radar" that can easily detect beliefs but fails to be attuned to habits; statements about ideas and concepts show up on this radar, but the rhythms and rituals of lived theology fail to make an

---

7. And if they do gravitate toward the suburbs, *should* they? Are there, in fact, aspects of evangelical faith and practice that should mitigate against that? And if they don't, why not?

appearance. Once again, this constitutes a narrow "theoretical gate" through which only a narrow bandwidth of "religion" makes it through. The other aspects that are not commensurate with this register (many of the aspects that attend embodiment, liturgy, practice) are thereby excluded from consideration.

Here again our project seeks to resist reductionistic approaches that tend to reduce religion to beliefs. Sociology of religion still tends to exhibit a Protestant bias that construes religion primarily in cognitive/propositional terms, as if religion was primarily a matter of beliefs and doctrines. But our sociological analysis is informed by a thicker understanding of human persons that understands them as creatures of habit and practice *before* they are thinking things or believing animals (cf. J. K. A. Smith 2008; 2009). Geographical habits are learned not didactically through the dissemination of ideas and doctrines, but subterraneously, through the inculcation of particular visions of "the good life" — "social imaginaries" — that are inscribed in us by affective means and "carried," as Charles Taylor puts it, in practices (Taylor 2004). Thus Christian Smith rightly describes the rituals and practices of "social life" as "liturgies": "All the social practices, relations, and institutions that comprise human social life generally themselves together dramatize, ritualize, proclaim, and reaffirm the moral order that constitutes social life" (C. Smith 2003, 16). Humans are the sorts of animals who absorb cultural teleologies and visions of the good life through rituals and practices that inscribe an orientation on and through the body in ways that usually elude conscious reflection. If our sociological register is calibrated only for the dissemination of "ideas," then we will miss some of the most important formative factors that shape and mold both religious imagination and geographical habits.

This requires not only a sociology attuned to the importance of practices (following Bourdieu), but also a theology that is primed to be attentive to the central role of formative practices. A sociology of practice tethered to a "talking head" theology will not do justice to the particularities of religious formation. In order to consider any correlation between evangelical spirituality and geographical habits, we will need a theological approach that considers the formative impact of affective practices.[8]

8 Here, studying a phenomenon like "evangelicalism" poses a unique challenge to congregational studies insofar as the amorphous character of evangelicalism is not easily tied to the boundaries of particular religious traditions/denominations, and not even to congregations. For instance, consideration of the formative practices of evangelicalism would have to attend not only to an ethnography of evangelical worship and liturgy but also

"Judicious Narratives" and the Disciplining of Ecclesiology

We have been suggesting a mutually enriching, mutually critical partnership between theology and social science with a view to discerning, understanding, and explaining correlations between evangelical spirituality (= theology and practice) and geographical habits. Theological claims need to be disciplined by sociological and ethnographic exposure to the empirical realities that push back against theological claims. And sociological observation needs to be calibrated so as to be attuned to the complexity and richness of social phenomena, particularly with respect to religious phenomena. Thus we share Christian Scharen's conviction (echoing Milbank) that theology needs sociology to supply "judicious narratives" that keep ecclesiology from floating off into the realm of the ideal (Scharen 2005). However, we have also tried to emphasize that sociology of religion needs theology to better inform its interests, questions, instruments, and observation in order to do justice to the particularities of congregational life.[9]

For our project this takes the form of qualitative research using instruments that are theologically informed while also providing space for stories to emerge. The narratives that emerge in qualitative research provide judicious witness of congregational realities "on the ground," encouraged by instruments that welcome the "thickness" of parishioners' theologically informed stories. In short, qualitative research provides a means for sociological observation that is commensurate with the cultural complexities we seek to study.

---

to a host of other institutions, including Christian radio, publishing, campus ministries, popular music, etc. "Formation" of the evangelical imagination spills far beyond the confines of the "congregation"; in fact, for many evangelicals, it seems, the *primary* sites of formation lie outside their congregational context.

9. Scharen's account understandably emphasizes the first, but not the second. Because of this it seems that, at times, he assumes some sociological axioms as givens (perhaps even "neutral," 130) that could then falsify theological claims (e.g., concerning the church/ world distinction, 133). He alludes to a "more complex understanding of culture" as a corrective to such naïve theological dichotomies, but such a "complex" understanding of culture does not seem to emerge. We think this is an important line of questioning and debate, but we do not think Scharen's critique has settled it. For instance, we do not think sociological accounts necessarily "falsify" supposedly "ideal" ecclesiologies precisely because it may be possible to articulate a "more complex" theory of culture that could account for and explain why ecclesial realities "on the ground" do not match up with the supposed "ideals." For further discussion, see J. K. A. Smith 2009, 208, n. 115.

Evangelicals and the City: A Case Study

Geographical Snapshot: Where Are Evangelicals?

As indicated above, there are three broad questions that orient our research: First, is the common perception of evangelicalism as a "suburban" religion warranted? Can the perception be solidified with social-scientific research? Second, if we can confirm a suburban "center of gravity" for evangelicalism, can we discern the causes of such, or at least discern key factors that might account for such a correlation? How do evangelicals tend to perceive the city? And why? How might we evaluate such a situation? Third, how might evangelicals think critically about both their anti-urban bias and their suburban location?

With respect to the first question, the concern is to get a rough-and-ready snapshot of how things look "on the ground." While fundamentalism was considered a rural religion (Singleton 1975 contests this somewhat), evangelicalism has often been considered a quintessentially suburban religious phenomenon. Robert Fishman's historical account traces much of the impetus for suburban development to the evangelical spirituality of the "Clapham sect" of Wilberforce et al. (Fishman 1987; cf. Hayden 2003; Mulder and Smith 2009). But does contemporary research support these common and historical intuitions? There are perhaps two ways to pose the question. On the one hand, one could ask how religious, or more specifically evangelical, the suburbs are. On this score, research seems to indicate that suburban Americans "are no more prone to religiosity than their urban counterparts" (Conn 1994, 98; Nash 1968; Newman 1976; Handy 1984). On the other hand we might ask how suburban evangelicals are; this is closer to our concern.

Despite an explosion of social-scientific interest in evangelicals over the past decade, questions of place and locale, particularly at the level of fine-grained distinctions between urban, suburban, and exurban, are rarely asked in such studies. However, there is some research that suggests evangelicals tend to be more often located in suburban contexts. While we do not have much data about where evangelical parishioners live, we do have some data about where evangelical *congregations* are located. Changes in the urban landscape over the twentieth century find expression in changes in the religious landscape at the same time.

In a study of Philadelphia congregations, Sinha et al. (2007) found that Catholic congregations were more likely to be "resident" congregations — that is, congregations in which 50 percent or more of members live within ten blocks of the congregation's building. "In fact, being a Catholic congregation was by far the biggest predictor (odds ratio of 3.9) of being a resident congregation, despite some relaxation of the requirement that Catholics attend the church within their parish" (Sinha et al. 2007, 251). In contrast, Baptist, Pentecostal, and nondenominational Christian congregations (all considered "evangelical" by RELTRAD [Religious Tradition]) made up more than half of "city commuter" congregations (253). However, the study cannot tell us whether evangelicals tend to suburban locations, because the Philadelphia Congregations Census was restricted to congregations within the city limits. Thus the study only considers suburban residents who commute to urban congregations.[10]

However, a recent study focused on individual parishioners rather than congregations confirms this suburban center-of-gravity for evangelicalism. "America's Evangelicals," a 2004 study conducted by John Green and Anna Greenberg, found that 25.4 percent of evangelicals surveyed lived in rural areas, whereas 31.9 percent lived in areas considered "urban," with the remaining 42.7 percent living in "suburban" and "exurban" social environments. Thus a higher percentage of evangelicals live in suburban/exurban contexts. However, when these numbers are considered with respect to race, the picture has notable characteristics: only 18.4 percent of white evangelicals live in urban areas, while 51.8 percent live in suburban/exurban contexts (just 29.8 percent live in rural areas). The situation is starkly different for black and Hispanic evangelicals: 68.9 percent of black evangelicals and 70.3 percent of Hispanic evangelicals live in urban areas, while only 18.5 percent of black evangelicals and 14 percent of Hispanic evangelicals live in suburban or exurban contexts.[11] The study also found

---

10. One of the reasons we lack solid data is that studies have not sufficiently distinguished urban from suburban. A study by Karnes et al. (2007) concerning the spatial distribution of megachurches — which are overwhelmingly evangelical — fails to provide information regarding any correlation between evangelicalism and anti-urban bias/suburban settlement because of a fuzzy and un-nuanced use of the term "urban." In other words, the study flies a bit too high and thus recognizes no significant difference between urban and suburban locales, categorizing entire metro areas as "urban." This same lack of nuance or distinction between urban and suburban makes it difficult to draw conclusions from Singleton's (1975) study of links between fundamentalism and urbanization.

11. Consideration of regional differences are illuminating and perhaps surprising. For instance, in the "Deep South" more evangelicals live in suburban/exurban contexts (37.4 percent) than rural (26.1 percent), whereas in the "West North Central" region 45.4 percent of evangelicals live in rural areas and only 37.1 percent live in suburban/exurban contexts.

an interesting contrast with other Christian traditions: the majority of mainline Protestants, like evangelicals, live in suburban and exurban contexts (45.5 percent), whereas more Roman Catholics (47.9 percent) live in urban areas (Green and Greenberg 2004).

Evangelical Perceptions of the City: A Qualitative Sketch

From the data available (and much more robust study is needed here), it seems fair to conclude that the common perception is not unwarranted: evangelicalism does seem to have a suburban "center of gravity," as it were. How does this correlate to their perceptions of the city?

It should be noted that our research found inspiration in Michael Emerson and Christian Smith's now decade-old *Divided by Faith: Evangelical Religion and the Problem of Race in America.* In that volume, Emerson and Smith articulated the ways in which evangelical spirituality and practice actually contributed to the racialization and segregation of American culture — the very antithesis of the picture of the redeemed community "from every nation, tribe, people and language" (Rev. 7:9).[12] Ours is a correlate (and supplementary) project that considers how white evangelicals tend to exhibit an anti-urban bias that contributes to a negative view of urban life and contributes to the growth of suburban and exurban social arrangements.

In an attempt to better understand white evangelical perceptions of the city, we undertook a line of inquiry that included 270 semistructured interviews with individuals attending various types of churches (evangelical, Roman Catholic, Mainline Protestant, and African American Protestant[13]) in both urban and suburban locations. In essence, we wanted to interview attenders in the following eight categories:

Suburban Evangelical
Urban Evangelical
Suburban Roman Catholic
Urban Roman Catholic

---

12. Emerson and Smith 2000.

13. We categorized congregational affiliation based on the RELTRAD. For our purposes, "Conservative Protestant" was synonymous with "evangelical." For more on this, see B. Steensland et al. 2000.

Suburban Mainline Protestant
Urban Mainline Protestant
Suburban African American Protestant
Urban African American Protestant

We utilized these eight categories in an effort to discern whether we could identify trends based on religious tradition, geography, or some combination of both. In essence, we wanted to discern whether something unique about evangelical spirituality pulled them toward suburbs. Using a snowball sampling method, the interviews were conducted over a two-year period from 2007 to 2009. Roughly, 230 of the interviews occurred with attenders of congregations from the Grand Rapids, Michigan metropolitan area. A subset of forty interviews were conducted with parishioners from congregations in other various regions of the United States. We then coded and analyzed the interview transcripts manually, utilizing QSR NVivo software.

From interviewing individuals from various religious traditions and geographical locations, a fairly complex picture emerges. We do, indeed, see some patterns that map onto religious traditions and others to geography. However, it should be noted that these trends are revealed in the manners in which the respondents actually discussed their thoughts about the city. In other words, the crux was not that the interviewees had negative or positive perceptions of the city. Rather, we found the language and stories that individuals employed to describe their perceptions revealed thicker reasoning for attitudes toward the city.

None of the cohorts of respondents from our eight categories offered uniform opinions regarding the city. However, patterns did emerge within the religious traditions. Respondents from all four religious traditions had negative perceptions of the city — white evangelicals were not alone in expressing a modicum of urban antipathy. However, further analysis of the responses revealed that different religious traditions tended to yield different concerns.

For instance, among African American Protestant attenders, the negative opinions most frequently had to do with matters of social injustice. That is, they more frequently referenced systems of injustice as the cause of urban problems. Respondents from both urban and suburban congregations would discuss issues related to gangs, crime, and teenage pregnancy, but typically only as a manifestation of deeper systemic ills. One man who attended what he described as an urban African Methodist church noted that "there are just more people than the safety net." A woman who attended an urban Missionary Baptist church offered a similar concern: "I think of, uh, the plight of inner-city schools. I think of the resources that are just draining from the city. I think of people in my age group, be they every race, that are leaving the city." Numerous other respondents from African American Protestant churches referenced broken city school systems as the most prominent issue that came to mind when considering negative aspects of the city. When discussing the negative aspects of the city, the attenders from African American Protestant congregations voiced concerns about structural injustice with much greater frequency than any of the cohorts from the three other religious traditions considered in this study.

In addition, it should be noted that interviewees from both urban and suburban African American Protestant congregations also frequently expressed positive sentiments about cities — these usually had to do with presence of diversity and something that we categorized as "opportunity/potential." When conducting analysis, we noticed that a number of respondents discussed urban areas as being places of exciting engagement — where institutions, like congregations, had venues for doing exciting work that might make for strong, vibrant communities. We concluded that these positive responses revealed a different type of appreciation than those that discussed entertainment, recreation, and conveniences (amenities) related to the city.

This distinction between opportunity/potential versus amenities also surfaced during interviews with individuals who attended mainline churches. These individuals seemed to have different positive notions based on where they attended church. When suburban mainline attenders discussed positive images of the city, it had to do with urban amenities: things to do downtown. When these same individuals discussed negative images, it often had to do with crime and poverty. In a marked distinction, when we analyzed the transcripts from the urban mainline attenders we saw much more positive discourse about the city. And not only was the quantity of positive discourse greater, the content of the conversation also tended to be different: while the suburban mainline attenders referenced the positive attributes in terms of amenities (entertainment, recreation, proximity), the urban mainline attenders offered much less detail about urban amenities. Instead, they tended to focus on issues that we coded — similar to attenders of African American churches — as opportunity/potential. A response from a male parishioner from an urban mainline congregation is indicative of the opportunity/potential code:

It really is, it's just that, I think we are called to the community and that's within the urban areas . . . I guess . . . the best quote would be at the end of the gospel it is "remain in the city," you know, Jesus says. Jesus leaves and he reminds his closest disciples . . . and he says stay in the city to receive the Holy Spirit. I think there's something to be said about urban life and if you look to the scriptures that we keep coming back to the development of community and get that mixed up because we keep thinking only of a family. . . .

By an overwhelming margin, urban mainline attenders discussed the positive attributes of the city by referencing not amenities, but opportunities for the development of vibrant authentic communities.

Perhaps our most surprising analysis occurred while considering the interview transcripts with Roman Catholic parishioners. The standard narrative[14] regarding church polity rightly asserts that the Catholic parish model leads to stronger connection between church and neighborhood. The close identity of parish and neighborhood, the geographical fixing of church responsibility, translated into Catholic churches remaining in their respective neighborhoods while white Protestant congregations moved with greater alacrity from urban neighborhoods that experienced racial transition. We had assumed that the parish structure, coupled with Catholic social justice teaching, would lead to interviews in which respondents articulated a strong sense of church-to-neighborhood connection and the significance of the city as a site for churches to be institutions that fomented social justice. Both cohorts (suburban and urban) of Roman Catholics discussed the city positively in terms of amenities: urban areas had structures in place to make for a more interesting life than in the suburbs. A man who attended an urban Catholic church summarizes:

Well, a city is a great place because it allows people to interact freely and quickly. So people can gather to their interests and minimize their transportation time. Interests that don't require a lot of space will take place in a city, so they are usually great generators of culture — they are encouraging to that. Certainly they are religious centers as well. Um . . . there is a lot of, for a young person, we would certainly want to be in a city-type setting because there is more of everything . . . more people, more opportunities, more education, and on and on. I really can't think of a lot of negative aspects associated with cities expect pol-

14. See McGreevy 1996; Gamm 1999.

lution and whatnot. Most cities . . . the amenities outweigh the negative aspects.

That type of positive urban perception related to amenities was mentioned among Catholics much more frequently than opportunity/potential. In terms of negative conceptions, we expected numerous references to cities being sites of social injustice. However, by a wide margin (and this is especially true of suburban Catholics) they discussed security issues more than social justice. A Catholic female elaborated: "The city? Violence. All the shootings. That kind of thing." In the end, the responses from Catholics surprised us in that they typically articulated a negative perception of the city that had more to do with fear of violence than frustrations because of social injustice.

While the analysis of the Catholic attenders failed to reveal any major difference between urban and suburban parishioners, we saw some tremendous difference between urban and suburban evangelicals as they discussed their respective opinions regarding the city. Overall, the suburban evangelicals articulated much more negative conceptions and tended to elaborate in ways that referenced issues of gangs, homelessness, violence, and nonfamily friendly aspects. One suburban evangelical woman described her fears:

> Um, as a petite female person who did not grow up in the city, my exposure to the city feels best when I'm in a group because I tend to wonder if I'm safe. And not being familiar and knowing what areas are fine for me to be alone in and what areas are not. So, I feel best if I am with people other than myself, so that's maybe a safety thing that comes to mind for me.

Another suburban evangelical woman offered similar sentiments about the city:

> Well, I guess it depends on where I am. Usually, I've never gone by myself to the city, you know usually large crowds. I usually feel really safe, but you know, if we're walking kind of on a side street or something, I'm like looking around my shoulder and you know kind of much more aware of what's going on around me, like, I do feel a little unsafe.

At a consistent rate, attenders from suburban evangelical congregations voiced concerns regarding safety issues in the urban context. Frequently, the respondents described apprehensions using codes such as "gangs," "crime," and "homelessness." It should be noted, though, that negative perceptions were not monolithic within the suburban evangelical interviews. In fact, many of the respondents indicated that they had positive impressions of the city. However, these positive statements overwhelmingly had to do with amenities. A typical suburban evangelical positive statement: "I think about Chicago, but I guess . . . lots of buildings and umm . . . companies, and people, busy people . . . and like arts and entertainment. Yeah. Trains and airports. . . ." In the end, the suburban evangelical tended to voice fairly stereotypical concerns about the city. When they discussed positive attributes, the content of the conversation frequently included mentions of entertainment and convenience (amenities).

In a striking contrast to the suburban evangelical interviews, the urban evangelical interviews offered a much less negative response to the concept of the city. In fact, the urban evangelical interviews displayed a striking absence of negative conceptions of the city when compared to the suburban evangelicals. Beyond that, when these two groups of evangelicals discuss the positive aspects of the city, they talk about different things. While the suburban evangelicals point to amenities, the urban evangelicals use language similar to urban mainline and both urban and suburban African American Protestant attenders: opportunity/potential. That is, the urban evangelicals seem tuned in to the potentiality of the city — that the future resides in the city, that it is a place of vibrancy and growth. Moreover (and more so than the urban mainline and African American attenders), the urban evangelicals frequently couch that opportunity/potential in theological terms. An attender from an urban evangelical congregation discussed how location of her place of worship forced some theological considerations:

> We have the school half a block from our house and it's a [local] public school. And there's never white kids walking to school. Well, our whole neighborhood is white, like where are these kids going to school? And so, all those kinds of issues come into play when you live in the city, whereas you live in the suburb, and it's all white kids walking to school, you don't think, well, where are the black kids? There are no black kids . . . or Hispanic or Asian or whatever. And too when I think about the city I think about the church and issues of race. The church I grew up in, they could ignore racism and not have it really affect them, whereas at [my church] you can't, it's in your face all the time. And you've got to learn, okay, what's my response going to be? And how is this going to inform how I think about the body of Christ?

An urban evangelical male also referenced theological concerns:

> Well, you know, there's some theological principles related to the city. Augustine sure sniffed it out. The city shows up in a lot of theological places. It's where people congregate. And, you know, it's the city where people are trying to be with people. Um, love God and neighbor, you know if you're not living in cities, your neighbor is an awful long ways away. My grandparents who were farmers lived in rural settings and their neighbors are a different concept of neighbor. Um, there's a sense that human beings need solitude, they need their downtime, but that only lasts for a short time, and we need, we need, people. So cities are there.

That type of theological reflection occurs frequently in the conversations with urban evangelical attenders and rarely with suburban evangelical attenders. When discussing the city, suburban evangelical attenders both praised the amenities and noted concerns about safety and a lack of family-friendliness — neither expression typically offered any theological elaboration. However, this is consonant with our methodological intuitions — that our relation to place is formed primarily at the level of unarticulated habits. It is not something we often make explicit (if ever), and thus questions that invite reflection on these issues are often trying to mine deep sensibilities that have never been articulated previously.

Analysis: Secular Liturgies, Congregational Practices, and Geographical Habits

A key finding here is that when suburban evangelicals discuss the city, they do so without theological reference. In contrast, urban evangelicals tend to reference the city in positive *theological* terms — in some ways, they actually sound like they have more in common with urban mainline attenders than their fellow evangelicals. And it is also important to remember that on a national scale, urban evangelicals are a significant minority: less than 20 percent of all white evangelicals. In other words, urban evangelicals often talk like "converts": they have had to reflect on place and their relation to cities in ways that have forced articulation. In contrast, suburban evangelicals have tended to "go with the flow," as it were; they have not thought about place and thus are more easily shaped and directed by status quo habit-forming practices.

From our ethnographic case study, it seems plausible to assume that at least part of the white evangelical proclivity for the suburbs has roots in theological *non*reflection. That is, choices about geographic habits are rarely brought under any type of theological interrogation; in other words, they might not be "choices" at all, but rather the sort of automatic outcomes of habits acquired through practices that operate below the radar of reflection. In short, many evangelicals — like many Americans more generally — fail to think critically about geography and location. In an echo of Emerson and Smith's argument regarding race, we see from these interviews that evangelical spirituality also has deep ramifications for attitudes regarding the city and geographical choices and habits.

This is instructive for the larger issue we are considering, namely, the adequacy of certain sociological methodologies for making sense of congregations and American religion. If actions are shaped and directed by rather "automated" habits and practices, then we might have lower expectations about what typical social-scientific instruments can tell us. There will be distinct limits to surveys and interviews precisely because they expect *articulation,* whereas the practices that significantly drive behavior carry implicit, unarticulated orientations to place. Further research on these themes, then, would have to pioneer an ethnography that carefully "reads" the practices of evangelical worship, as well as other suburban "secular liturgies," in order to determine how our orientation to place, especially cities, is shaped and primed. And such work would require important partnerships between ecclesiology and ethnography to properly understand contemporary religious phenomena.

References

Bakke, Ray. 1987. *The Urban Christian.* Downers Grove, IL: InterVarsity Press.

Bobinac, Ankica Marinovic. 1999. "Urbanost pentekostalnih zajednica: socio-demografska obiljezja zagrebackih pentekostalaca [Urbanity of pentecostal communities: Socio-demographic characteristics of Zagreb pentecostals]." *Sociologija sela* 37: 407-27.

Claerbaut, David. 1983. *Urban Ministry.* Grand Rapids: Zondervan.

Conn, Harvie M. 1994. *The American City and the Evangelical Church: A Historical Overview.* Grand Rapids: Baker Books.

Diamond, Etan. 2003. *Souls of the City: Religion and the Search for Community in Postwar America.* Bloomington: Indiana University Press.

Ellison, Craig W., and Edward S. Maynard. 1992. *Healing for the City: Counseling in the Urban Setting.* Grand Rapids: Zondervan.

Emerson, Michael O., and Christian Smith. 2000. *Divided by Faith: Evangelical Religion and the Problem of Race in America.* Oxford: Oxford University Press.

Fer, Yannick. 2007. "Pentecôtisme et modernité urbaine: Entre déterritorialisation des identities et réinvestissement symbolique de l'espace urbain." *Social Compass* 54: 201-10.

Finke, Roger, and Rodney Stark. 2005. *The Churching of America, 1776-2005: Winners and Losers in the Religious Economy.* New Brunswick, NJ: Rutgers University Press.

Fishman, Robert. 1987. *Bourgeois Utopias: The Rise and Fall of Suburbia.* New York: Basic Books.

Gamm, Gerald. 1999. *Urban Exodus: Why the Jews Left Boston and the Catholics Stayed.* Cambridge, MA: Harvard University Press.

Green, John, and Anna Greenberg. 2004. "America's Evangelicals." Available at http://www.thearda.com/Archive/Files/Descriptions/EVANGEL.asp.

Handy, Robert T. 1984. *A Christian America: Protestant Hopes and Historical Realities.* New York: Oxford University Press.

Hayden, Dolores. 2003. *Building Suburbia: Green Fields and Urban Growth, 1820-2000.* New York: Pantheon Books.

Hudnut-Beumler, James. 1994. *Looking for God in the Suburbs: The Religion of the American Dream and Its Critics, 1945-1965.* New Brunswick, NJ: Rutgers University Press.

Hunt, Tristram. 2005. *Building Jerusalem: The Rise and Fall of the Victorian City.* New York: Metropolitan Books/Henry Holt and Company.

Jackson, Kenneth T. 1985. *Crabgrass Frontier: The Suburbanization of the United States.* New York: Oxford University Press.

Karnes, Kimberly, W. McIntosh, I. L. Morris, and S. Pearson-Merkowitz. 2007. "Mighty Fortresses: Explaining the Spatial Distribution of American Megachurches." *Journal for the Scientific Study of Religion* 46: 261-68.

Kenneson, Philip D. 1999. *Beyond Sectarianism: Re-imagining Church and World.* Valley Forge, PA: Trinity Press International.

Marsh, Margaret. 2007. "Urban View and Suburban Landscapes: A Twenty-First-Century Assessment of the History of Metropolitan Development." *Journal of Urban History* 33: 645-51.

McGreevy, John T. 1996. *Parish Boundaries: The Catholic Encounter with Race in the Twentieth Century Urban North.* Chicago: The University of Chicago Press.

Milbank, John. 1990. *Theology and Social Theory: Beyond Secular Reason*. Oxford: Blackwell.

Mulder, Mark T., and James K. A. Smith. 2009. "Subdivided by Faith? An Historical Account of Evangelicals and the City." *Christian Scholar's Review* 38: 415-33.

Mulder, Mark T., and James K. A. Smith. 2010. "Making Sense of Church." *Perspectives* 25.3: 5-6.

Nash, Dennison. 1968. "And a Little Child Shall Lead Them: A Test of an Hypothesis That Children Were the Source of the American 'Religious Revival.'" *Journal for the Scientific Study of Religion* 7: 238-40.

Newman, William M. 1976. "Religion in Suburban America." In *The Changing Face of the Suburbs*, edited by Barry Schwartz, pp. 267-68. Chicago: University of Chicago Press.

Nicolaides, Becky. 2006. "How Hell Moved from the City to the Suburbs: Urban Scholars and Changing Perceptions of Authentic Community." In *The New Suburban History*, edited by Kevin M. Kruse and Thomas J. Sugrue, pp. 80-98. Chicago: University of Chicago Press.

Perella, F. J., Jr. 1996. "Roman Catholic Approaches to Urban Ministry, 1945-1985." In *Churches, Cities, and Human Community: Urban Ministry in the United States, 1945-1985*, edited by C. J. Green, pp. 179-211. Grand Rapids: Eerdmans.

Ramsay, Meredith. 1998. "Redeeming the City: Exploring the Relationship between Church and Metropolis." *Urban Affairs Review* 33: 595-626.

Scharen, Christian B. 2005. "'Judicious Narratives,' or Ethnography *as* Ecclesiology." *Scottish Journal of Theology* 58: 125-42.

Sharlet, Jeff. 2005. "Inside America's Most Powerful Megachurch." *Harper's* (May): 41-54.

Sharp, Elaine B. 2007. "Revitalizing Urban Research: Can Cultural Explanation Bring Us Back from the Periphery?" *Urban Affairs Review* 43: 55-75.

Shaw, Iain J. 2002. *High Calvinism in Action: Calvinism and the City, Manchester and London, c. 1810-1860*. Oxford: Oxford University Press.

Singleton, Gregory. 1975. "Fundamentalism and Urbanization: A Quantitative Critique of Impressionistic Interpretations." In *The New Urban History*, edited by Leo Schnore, pp. 205-27. Princeton: Princeton University Press.

Sinha, Jill Witmer, A. Hillier, Ram A. Cnaan, and C. C. McGrew. 2007. "Proximity Matters: Exploring Relationships among Neighborhoods, Congregations, and the Residential Patterns of Members." *Journal for the Scientific Study of Religion* 46: 245-60.

Smith, Christian. 2003. *Moral, Believing Animals: Human Personhood and Culture.* New York: Oxford University Press.

Smith, James K. A. 1999. "Liberating Religion from Theology: Marion and Heidegger on the Possibility of a Phenomenology of Religion." *International Journal for Philosophy of Religion* 46: 17-33.

Smith, James K. A. 2004. *Introducing Radical Orthodoxy: Mapping a Postsecular Theology.* Grand Rapids: Baker Academic.

Smith, James K. A. 2008. "Philosophy of Religion Takes Practice: Liturgy as Source and Method in Philosophy of Religion." In *Contemporary Method and Practice in Philosophy of Religion,* edited by D. Cheetham and R. King. London: Continuum.

Smith, James K. A. 2009. *Desiring the Kingdom: Worship, Worldview, and Cultural Formation.* Cultural Liturgies, 1. Grand Rapids: Baker Academic.

Steensland, Brian, J. Z. Park, M. D. Regnerus, L. D. Robinson, W. B. Wilcox, and R. D. Woodberry. 2000. "The Measure of American Religion: Toward Improving the State of the Art." *Social Forces* 79: 291-318.

Taylor, Charles. 2004. *Modern Social Imaginaries.* Durham, NC: Duke University Press.

Wilson, Timothy D. 2002. *Strangers to Ourselves: Discovering the Adaptive Unconscious.* Cambridge, MA: Harvard University Press.

Winston, Diane. 1998. "Babylon by the Hudson; Jerusalem on the Charles: Religion and the American City." *Journal of Urban History* 25: 122-29.

Winter, Gibson. 1961. *The Suburban Captivity of the Churches: An Analysis of Protestant Responsibility in the Expanding Metropolis.* Garden City, NY: Doubleday.

Wolterstorff, Nicholas. 1983. *Until Justice and Peace Embrace.* Grand Rapids: Eerdmans.

CHAPTER 6

Ethnography as Ecclesial Attentiveness and Critical Reflexivity: Fieldwork and the Dispute over Homosexuality in the Episcopal Church

Christopher Craig Brittain

In contemporary debates over the relationship between theology and the social sciences, theologians frequently sound a defensive alarm. Some ecclesiologists, for example, warn that the discipline of ecclesiology is properly an inquiry about God, and ought not to be reduced to mere socio-historical description of a particular church community. Such a caution is generally accompanied by a series of examples of supposedly "theological" reflections on the church, which only narrate its contextual history and offer the latest demographic data. These illustrations are usually supplied by the concerned theologian to add weight to the accusation that theology and social science ought not to mix.

The marshaling of such "empirical evidence" on the dangers of any partnership between theology and social-scientific investigation is complemented by a growing literature in systematic theology about the dangerous potential for social theory to colonize the discipline. Such a warning found its manifesto in the form of John Milbank's influential book *Theology and Social Theory*. Modern theology, he argues, has been guilty of a "false humility" before the social sciences, and has passively submitted itself to being governed by the methodologies and truth claims of secular reason. In his view, granting independent authority to social science erodes the distinctiveness of theology's proper task and its object. Furthermore, such a perspective fails to recognize "that 'scientific' social theories are themselves theologies or antitheologies in disguise."[1]

---

1. John Milbank, *Theology and Social Theory* (Oxford: Blackwell, 1990), p. 3.

Milbank's appeal for theology to avoid any dependence on social science can be understood as a reaction against what he saw as a dominant trend in the theology of the 1980s in Britain, but also Western Europe and North America. On the one hand, he was concerned to challenge methods of correlation, which followed positions similar to those developed by Paul Tillich and David Tracy.[2] He was perhaps even more alarmed by the popularity of Latin American Liberation Theology, with its emphasis on contextual *praxis* and critiques of traditional theology from "the underside."[3] In such approaches to the study of the church, Milbank and others have worried that theology was losing its sense that to speak *theologically* of the church was to speak of God. Rather than investigating the church's origin in the movement and work of the divine, ecclesiology was simply describing particular measurable phenomena found within contemporary communities who happen to call themselves "Christian." One should admit that it is not terribly difficult to find examples of the kind of ecclesiology and "theological reflection" of the sort that worries these critics of the use of social-scientific methodologies by theologians. But does this mean that this is the inevitable outcome of such a partnership?

This chapter makes a case for both the appropriateness and significance of the use of sociological methods in ecclesiology, with particular attention to ethnography. This defense of the contribution of social-scientific methodology to theology is developed with reference to a particular concrete problem confronting contemporary mainline Christian churches: the possibility of schism over the issue of homosexuality. The Church of Scotland is currently experiencing serious tensions and division over the recognition of a gay pastor serving in a congregation in Aberdeen. At the same time, the Anglican Communion is confronted with a similar controversy, in the form of the consecration of two gay bishops in the Episcopal Church of the United States, along with the blessing of same sex-unions in a number of Anglican Provinces. Some congregations, and even full dioceses, have split with their local church, and many more threaten to do the same. As an Anglican, this is of considerable concern to me.

There has been a great deal of ink spilled on the issue of homosexuality in biblical studies, as well as in systematic theology. What is noteworthy, however, is how little this literature helps resolve the ongoing conflict in

---

2. See, for example, Paul Tillich, *Theology of Culture* (Oxford: Oxford University Press, 1964); Paul Tracy, *Blessed Rage for Order* (Chicago: University of Chicago Press, 1996).

3. See Gustavo Gutiérrez, *The Theology of Liberation* (London: SCM Press, 1991).

the churches over this question. There is even evidence of an exhausted, or even cynical, attitude toward the possibility that theology has any possible contribution to make to mediate the dispute. Oliver O'Donovan has lamented, "Faced with yet another attempt to get at the meaning of *arsenokites* [male prostitute? sodomite? homosexual?] by philology, I cry: Enough!"[4] Many members of the Church of Scotland, as well as in the different Anglican churches throughout the world, have spent years listening to debates and arguments over the question of homosexuality. Studies have been commissioned, discussion groups formed, and "listening processes" implemented. These ecclesial attempts to "move the debate forward" have indeed helped to educate church members about the differing theological, biblical, and scientific positions on the issue; what they have not done, however, is achieve consensus. More to the point, such processes have not prevented some churches from discovering that disagreement over the question has brought them to the point where serious institutional fragmentation is a real possibility.

This failure on the part of systematic theology and biblical studies to resolve the debate in the church over homosexuality suggests there is more to learn about the nature of this conflict. Deeper understanding of this division in the church is required if ecclesiology is to better grasp what God would have the church do in the present situation, and what it might mean to be "church" in the midst of such a dispute. It is at this point that a role for social-scientific study in ecclesiology comes into view. There is a "practical" side to the present need for theological reflection on the conflict over homosexuality, for many questions confront the church that merit greater understanding, and failure to answer these questions will have substantial consequences. Why is it that the current theological arguments on offer are not sufficient to achieve relative consensus? What understandings of church are implied by the way this conflict is understood by its members, and by the ways in which the ecclesial leadership seeks to "manage" it? What impact is the ongoing tension over this issue having on church members, as well as on the witness of the denomination to the external world? These are significant ecclesiological questions that can be more adequately considered by attending to the concrete actions and attitudes found within and among Christians in these church congregations.

---

4. Oliver O'Donovan, "Homosexuality in the Church: Can There Be a Fruitful Theological Debate?" in *Theology and Sexuality,* ed. Eugene F. Rogers Jr. (Oxford: Blackwell, 2002), pp. 379-80.

Given that "human experience is a 'place' where the gospel is grounded, embodied, interpreted and lived out," empirical study of congregational life serves to illuminate how different Christians are working out their faith in the context of the painful disputes over homosexuality.[5] Without some knowledge of the particularity of these present embodiments of the gospel, the church will be less able to understand itself in the current historical moment, and so ecclesiology will remain substantially impoverished during a moment of crisis. To illustrate how such empirical study can contribute to the work of understanding what God might be doing in the context of the church — the proper *theological* focus of ecclesiology — this chapter offers some examples of how an ethnographic study I am currently engaged in might contribute to an ecclesiological understanding of the dispute within the Anglican Communion.

The Conflict over Homosexuality in the Anglican Communion

Since the mid-1990s, the global Anglican Communion has been caught up in an increasingly intense conflict over the role of gays and lesbians in the church. In 2002, the synod of the Diocese of New Westminster in western Canada passed a motion in favor of public rites for blessing same-sex unions. A number of conservatives walked out of the synod. It was in 2003, however, that the situation erupted into a full crisis, when openly gay candidates were put forward as the bishops of New Hampshire and of Reading in the Diocese of Oxford. After a considerable controversy within the Church of England, Jeffrey Johns withdrew his name, but the consecration of Gene Robinson as Bishop of New Hampshire was approved by the General Assembly of The Episcopal Church (TEC). Such was the ongoing rancor that several hundred bishops boycotted the Lambeth 2008 meetings, many of whom attended an alternative meeting in Jerusalem, called the Global Anglican Futures Conference (GAFCON).

Discontent in North America and England has led some theologians to follow the path trod by John Henry Newman into the Roman Catholic Church, echoing his lament over the dangers of modern relativism. In the United States, R. R. Reno has reversed an earlier plea to resist the tempta-

---

5. John Swinton and Harriet Mowat, *Practical Theology and Qualitative Research* (London: SCM Press, 2006), p. 5.

tion to move from Canterbury to Rome. He now argues that "We cannot move through the spiritual life the way we drift through the marketplace. Dogma and the sacramental system must define and circumscribe our belief." In the absence of doctrinal clarity, Reno concludes, "the Episcopal Church is disastrously disordered and disarrayed."[6] Within the Anglican Church of Canada, Douglas Farrow has made a similar conclusion, insisting that Anglicanism has "run aground."[7] Some prominent African bishops have accused both North American national churches, but also the Church of England, of abandoning the authority of Scripture and the traditions of the church by failing to condemn homosexuality in sufficiently clear terms. The final report of the GAFCON conference denounced "the acceptance and promotion within the provinces of the Anglican Communion of a different 'gospel' (cf. Gal. 1:6-8) which is contrary to the apostolic gospel." As a consequence of this disagreement over homosexuality, the bishops present at this conference declared themselves to be "out of communion" with those who promote such a "false gospel."[8] Some African bishops have sent "missionary" priests and bishops into the dioceses of TEC to represent the "true" version of the Anglican faith, causing considerable controversy at both the local and the international level.

However one might interpret the intensity of reactions against the idea of welcoming same-sex relationships into the churches of the Anglican Communion, it is clear that the boundaries of this controversy have expanded into a debate over the very theological integrity of Anglicanism itself. Philip Turner argues that Anglican theology has become "unworkable." He suggests that "the Episcopal Church's problem is far more theological than it is moral — a theological poverty that is truly monumental and that stands behind the moral missteps recently taken by its governing bodies."[9] Other Anglican theologians have responded by emphasizing that the Anglican tradition has always been diverse, but that it has sought to make room to include differing views and practices. Paul Avis, suggesting that the controversy is a distraction from more central concerns of the Christian faith, laments, "Anglicans should have a bad conscience about

6. R. R. Reno, "Out of the Ruins," *First Things* 150 (February 2005): 16.

7. Douglas Farrow, "Anglicanism Runs Aground," *First Things* 149 (January 2005): 11-13.

8. "Statement of the Global Anglican Future," GAFCON final statement (Jerusalem, 29 June 2008), available at: http://www.gafcon.org/news/gafcon_final_statement/ (accessed 13 November 2010).

9. Philip Turner, "An Unworkable Theology," *First Things* 154 (June/July 2005): 10.

squandering energy on internal squabbles while God yearns to redeem the world."[10]

The principal institutional way that the leadership of the Anglican Communion has sought to deal with this controversy has been to issue documents like the *Windsor Report* in 2004, which calls upon all parties to cease hostilities and controversial activities (ordaining gay priests, blessing same-sex relationships, and invading the jurisdiction of other bishops). The report also calls for further theological study and for the establishment of an "Anglican Covenant," a statement of agreement and fellowship that continues to be controversial and under development. As these policy documents are being drafted and debated, numerous acts of schism have continued to develop. In the United States, the diocese of San Joaquin formally withdrew from the Episcopal Church in 2007. In 2008, the dioceses of Pittsburgh, Dallas/Fort Worth, and Quincy followed, formally supported by the Primate of the Province of the Southern Cone (South America) as well as numerous African churches. The Anglican Communion has begun to internally fragment.

Analyses of Anglican ecclesiology have to date proven unable to resolve this developing crisis in the church, for the very nature of what it means to be "church" has been one of the stakes in the battle. Neither have documents like the *Windsor Report* been able to cool the tensions between differing groups.[11] Given the seemingly irreconcilable divisions between the differing parties, a fruitful way for ecclesiology to proceed is to put less emphasis, at least temporarily, on declarations and normative claims about the church, and to begin a careful and attentive ethnographic study of the conflict. For it remains far from clear why differences within the Anglican churches, which have been in existence for decades, seemingly can no longer be tolerated, so that member churches feel unable to coexist within the same ecclesial framework. The following is a summary of work in progress from two different ethnographic projects, one focused on bishops within the four national churches in Great Britain, and the other located within five congregations in the (now two) dioceses of Pittsburgh.

---

10. Paul Avis, "Anglican Ecclesiology," in *Routledge Companion to the Christian Church*, ed. Gerard Mannion and Lewis Seymour Mudge (London: Routledge, 2003), p. 203.

11. For an analysis of the *Windsor Report*'s attempt to employ a concept of "core doctrine" to deal with the crisis, see Christopher Craig Brittain, "Confession Obsession," *Anglican Theological Review* 90, no. 4 (2008): 777-99.

The Situation in the Communion according to British Bishops

Over the past two years, my colleague Andrew McKinnon (Sociology, Aberdeen University) and I have interviewed twenty bishops in Britain, conducting semistructured interviews focused on the present crisis in the Anglican Communion. There was near unanimity expressed among the bishops in our sample that the conflict was not solely about homosexuality, and most tended to think the conflict was not even *primarily* about sexuality. More than half of the bishops used the same metaphor to talk about the crisis, describing homosexuality as the "presenting issue," "presenting problem," or "presenting symptom," to describe an illness in the "Body of Christ." While there may be widespread agreement about the secondary nature of this particular symptom, this does not mean that the bishops agree among themselves on what the underlying disease is, or how it ought to be treated.

Having explained why he is convinced that homosexuality is wrong, incompatible with Scripture and with Christian faith, Bishop John argued that those within the church who are advocating blessing same-sex unions, or allowing for practicing gay and lesbian clergy and bishops, are effectively changing the gospel:

> So in a sense the very real issue: the debate in the church isn't about homosexuality at all. Homosexuality is the presenting problem. I think we all wish it was a different one but it's the presenting problem of how seriously we take the authority of the Bible and especially of how seriously we are committed to the faith of the apostles.

Bishop Luke, who is in favor of full inclusion, also used the language of the "presenting issue." He argued that in the Anglican Communion there are deep cultural differences around the issue of homosexuality. Nevertheless, he argued, the conflict is far from simply a product of cross-cultural differences. In Britain and North America, he explains,

> you have conservative reactions — though it isn't the same sort of cultural reactions. . . . It then seems to suggest the church is abandoning its historic traditions. And so, all the other issues about the authority of Scripture, what the church has historically taught, the understanding of marriage. . . . It seems that suddenly in giving way pastorally to the needs of gay and lesbian people, you're running a coach and horses through the whole tradition, so people get very anxious about it. So,

apart from the personal issues, you get both positive and negative reactions because people have got agendas of their own.

You've got all those other issues. So it's become a political issue. It's
a campaigning issue. So it's the presenting issue for a battle for power
in the church.

The bishops recognized the "symbolic" nature of the dispute, insofar as
"homosexuality" in this conflict largely stands for something else, even as
there is considerable disagreement about what that something is. Several
of the bishops argued, in different ways, that the symbolic nature of this
conflict is one of the primary reasons it seems so intractable. Bishop Timothy makes a comparison with the conflict in Northern Ireland, where
tough legislation had swept away political patronage, and resulted in substantial change. But, he explains,

> what trips you up is the symbolic stuff because that's the enduring
> stuff: "I have walked down that road for the last 150 years." . . . [These
> may not be issues of substance but] they have a visceral connection
> with identity . . . with who people are. So they're not negotiable. And I
> guess that in some elements the gay issue has become symbolic, which
> means that they're not negotiable.

One bishop, who considers himself an "open" Evangelical, lamented the
way in which his wing of the church had become increasingly divided between more moderate (or "liberal") Evangelicals and hard-line conservatives. These conservative evangelicals tend to see themselves as the heirs to
the Puritans, who never got their chance to "complete the Reformation."
As Bishop David explains,

> all Anglicans will say that the Bible is our fundamental authority. . . .
> Evangelicals will almost stop there even though they are paying lip
> service to tradition and reason. . . . And then classic Anglicanism will
> talk about the Bible interpreted through tradition and with the use of
> reason and taking into account experience. . . . There are a number of
> ways of configuring that ground. But all of us would start with the Bi-
> ble. But of course the conservative evangelical will be suspicious of
> what everybody else means by the authority of the Bible. And that
> suspicion eventually has led to: "Okay, let's test it out, let's see what
> they mean by this." And the feeling of having perhaps retreated and
> been sucked into the church as a whole has now been challenged:

> "Okay, let's see what the color of their money is and what they really mean by the authority of the Bible." And then you run into the hermeneutical questions. . . . You've got this one issue taken as a litmus test for . . . liberalism.

When we suggested that it is often most difficult to hold a position in the middle as an issue gets increasingly polarized, Bishop David expressed a considerable amount of exasperation.

> I think that's right! Of much more concern, and this is part of that, is that we don't seem to be able to discuss in that area now. A banner is raised, a word is said, a phrase is used and you know immediately which side of this divide you're on. And people listen out for trigger phrases, for symbolic phrases and words. So that middle area of intellectual debate, of real honest grappling, is getting evacuated as people just make it into a political scrap instead of a theological debate. I think Rowan Williams is classically one of those people who gets castigated from both sides as he tries to hold us together. What I'm saying is that we need to be able, within Anglicanism, to have the big tent that allows us to have the same tools and reach different conclusions with integrity and to live with that integrity of difference. Why this issue, for instance? There are seven texts on this issue and two thousand verses on poverty in the Bible. So I say, "For heaven sake, don't make this a Communion-breaking issue."

Bishop David here explains the way that the symbol of homosexuality marks a divide, or better, constructs a divide between those who "really" accept the authority of the scriptures, and those whose orthodoxy, and even the authenticity of their Christian faith, is questionable. By making the question of gays in the church the "litmus test" of orthodoxy, the boundaries of the Evangelical wing of the church are redrawn; it becomes very difficult for Anglicans who think of themselves as part of the Evangelical wing of the church, who do not share the view that such an issue ought to be the dividing line between authentic Christians and apostates.

When we interviewed Evangelicals on the other side of the homosexuality issue, they also found the idea of "real" Evangelicals who could take a different view of the seven biblical texts thought to refer to homosexuality difficult to comprehend. Bishop John even seemed a bit surprised at the suggestion when it was put to him:

I think the issue is that I can cope with somebody that's a Christian seeking to be equally faithful to the Bible as I'm trying to be and who comes to a different conclusion but really wants to take the Bible seriously and argues on the basis of the Bible and says that I haven't understood it properly. I might disagree with them but I can take that. But what I think is very difficult is for them to say, "I am a Christian and I respect the authority of the Bible," but in a very cavalier manner, "I'm willing to dismiss the plain teaching of the Bible and 2000 years of the history of the church on holiness."

Although he knows other Evangelical bishops who do not see the issue as one that must divide the wheat from the chaff, Bishop John is only able to see such a position as "cavalier," and a dismissal of both Scripture and tradition, rather than something about which Evangelicals could — and do in fact — disagree.

Like Bishop John, Bishop Daniel explains that in his view, fellow Evangelicals who want to argue that homosexuality is not a sin in the Bible would have to ignore "two thousand years of interpretation," and allow that tradition to be relativized by "contemporary knowledge, contemporary experience, validating or giving of authority to contemporary experience is a constant argument within Anglicanism with [Richard] Hooker's language of Scripture, tradition, and reason."

While Bishop Daniel uses the traditional Anglican formulation, whereby Scripture, tradition, and reason each ought all to be considered in light of the others, he downplays "contemporary" reason and "contemporary" experience compared with a supposedly uniform way that the church has read Scripture (at least on the issue of same-sex sexual relations) over the course of two millennia.

This "Catholicizing" of Evangelicals within the Anglican churches is somewhat surprising, given the past hundred and fifty years of tensions between the two groups. In England Anglo-Catholics have, in the past several decades, objected vociferously to women priests, and more recently, to women bishops, but, with a few notable exceptions, have made very little noise about homosexuality in the church. The Evangelicals have been more supportive of the question of women priests and bishops, but have been more likely to be opposed to greater inclusion of gays and lesbians. The Anglo-Catholics have leaned the other way, as one bishop (not an Anglo-Catholic) explains: "The Anglo-Catholic tradition, with its emphasis on ritual, on vestments, and so forth, has always tended to be a bit camp, and they've always been quite open on the question of homosexuality, even if they haven't on women's ordination" (Bishop Mathew). Another suggested that "the [Anglo-]Catholic wing is absolutely riddled with [homosexuality]. This is an agenda that they just don't want to talk about, for obvious reasons. Women are the issue. They can't deal with the gay issue, because the gay issue comes right close to home" (Bishop Luke). This is not really true outside of the United Kingdom, where (conservative) Anglo-Catholics have been an important constituent part of the protest against the elevation of Gene Robinson, particularly within the U.S. Several of the dioceses where there was the fiercest reaction to Gene Robinson (San Joaquin, San Antonio, Quincy) are strongly Anglo-Catholic dioceses, and have been the remaining holdouts to women's ordination within the Episcopal Church.

Several of the bishops talked about a "surprising" new alliance between conservative Anglo-Catholics and conservative evangelicals, particularly in North America, but also, though to a lesser extent, in England, where they have created strategic partnerships because of their shared opposition to the "liberal agenda." At the same time, "they're very different in the concerns they have about the liberal agenda" (Bishop Peter). Not only are their specific anxieties different, but so too their style of being Anglican. The GAFCON experience was marked by "the astonishment of Evangelicals, who are not used to any liturgy, or robes, or anything like that. Suddenly they find themselves in a high church liturgy, both conservative African and high church Catholic and others, where the host is being elevated" (Bishop David). Of the two GAFCON participants that we have interviewed in the project to date, one, an Evangelical, emphasized the great unity among the "orthodox Anglicans," or "historic, orthodox Anglicans" who participated in the event. The other, a conservative Anglo-Catholic, was somewhat less sanguine. He suggested that among the conservative dissidents,

> I think there is tension. For instance, there were people [at GAFCON] who ordained women and people there who didn't ordain women. And the declaration itself recognizes it and says that you work through those kinds of things. Whether the tension will be greater than the need for unity is the question. I don't know the answer to that. But yes, undoubtedly, people who are in some ways unlike each other now see the need to hang together. (GAFCON participant 2)

The Jerusalem declaration was produced as the key statement emerging from the GAFCON conference in Jerusalem. Rather than simply being the expression of a self-evident "Anglican Orthodoxy," this is a compromise document, an attempt to *create* Anglican Orthodoxy by means of compromise between conservative evangelicals and conservative Anglo-Catholics, each of whom have historically emphasized different (and even contradictory) elements of the Anglican tradition. The formulation of the Jerusalem declaration on the Bible betrays this attempt to suture together the two traditions: "The Bible is to be translated, read, preached, taught and obeyed in its plain and canonical sense, respectful of the church's historic and consensual reading" (GAFCON 2008 no. 2). It is far from obvious that the Evangelicals' "plain sense" and the Catholics' canonical, historic, and consensual readings mean the same thing, or are so readily reconciled with one another.

Among conservatives, the designation "liberal" is often presented as a self-evident designation. For those who are so marked, the category is not nearly so obvious. Bishop David, who identifies himself an Evangelical, feels that he is often discredited by his fellow religionists because he sees homosexuality as a matter that is *adiaphora,* an issue over which there can legitimately be disagreement in the church. Describing the response of some of his fellow Evangelicals to his attempt to avoid the polarizing terms of the debate on homosexuality, he says, "I think it's sometimes the case that someone you think has been in your tribe, and then actually you find has moved a bit, then you're more suspicious and angry with them than you are with somebody who has never been in the tribe to begin with." It may be, however, that whether one is in or out of the "tribe" depends on what boundary markers are currently in place. When different issues are used to distinguish insiders from outsiders, the whole configuration of what counts as inside and what counts as outside changes. It may well be that the boundaries have moved far more than Bishop David has.

Bishop Kevin expressed some doubt about whether "liberal" was a meaningful designation outside of the parameters of the current conflict, and whether such a group has been identified by the new alliance of conservative evangelicals and conservative Anglo-Catholics. He asks,

> to what extent is "liberalism" an invented category that allows these folks to gather, and ignore their own differences? To what extent is it the straw man that they've erected to legitimize their own struggle for control of the church? When I ask people "What is a liberal, in your view?" I get a thousand different answers, except that they're bad people, and not real Christians. We've placed ourselves outside the church,

and all this. Now if I were just to speak personally, I would be, I suppose, a liberal on the sexuality issue, but I'm not a liberal on a *whole* lot of other things. I'm not a liberal liturgically. . . . I'm not a liberal — I get letters from priests in the diocese wanting to throw the communion table open to everybody, baptized or not. And I say, "You cannot do that. The Eucharist is the meal of the baptized." And, there's a lot of pressure on language, and language change, and I am not liberal about that. So I don't really know if I am a liberal, or what one is. So, I suspect it's a kind of invention, and one of the difficulties in this discussion is stereotyping, and of course it happens in all directions. I'm not saying that only conservatives do stereotyping.

The conservatives might provide "a thousand different answers" for why they would identify Bishop Kevin as a "liberal" (and there is little doubt that they do), but there is one clear point of agreement between Bishop Kevin and his conservative interlocutors: that the distinction between the groups is most clearly marked by where one stands on the question of homosexuality. This has become the most salient symbol of the conflict, a hook onto which conservatives have managed to hang a number of different complaints, and which liberals use to simplify the concerns of conservatives. It serves as a salient marker that, in the view of those aligning themselves with GAFCON, separates the sheep from the goats and the wheat from the chaff.

The results of these interviews suggest a number of issues for consideration by any ecclesiological reflections among Anglicans. It would seem that the conflict over homosexuality is in the process of redrawing the boundaries within the churches of the Anglican Communion, although it is impossible to say what the lasting implications of this will be. Even if the conflict is not about sexual orientation per se, homosexuality has become the most salient symbol of the conflict, and a marker that constructs a divide: "liberals" and "conservatives." Although such observations must necessarily be tentative, the "homosexuality" marker is fueling an attempt to unite Anglo-Catholic and Evangelical constituencies, as well as contributing to the formation of a new identity, "Orthodox Anglicanism." Whether either the divisions within Anglo-Catholic and Evangelical communities or the suturing of the conservative communities will be successful in the long run, only time will tell.

The coalition is built on what could be described as a potentially unstable theological alliance, premised mostly on a shared common enemy.

Whether this will be sufficient to hold them together, particularly as they separate from the institutions they see as dominated by liberals (the Anglican Church of Canada, and the Episcopal Church), remains to be seen. There are real sources of latent tension, including not only styles of worship, but matters of doctrine. The Evangelicals will likely have difficulty with Anglo-Catholic emphases on the doctrine of the church and the nature of the sacraments, their warmth of feeling toward Rome, the place of Mary, and their high view of the orders of ministry. The Anglo-Catholics may find more charismatic forms of worship, a particular emphasis and hermeneutic toward Scripture (largely devoid of reference to the Church Fathers) problematic, as well as the fact that many Evangelicals support the ordination of women to both the priesthood and the episcopate. A further potential "deal breaker" is that in some of the "lowest" Evangelical Anglican churches (especially in Sydney, Australia) there is considerable support for laypeople presiding at the Eucharist.

It is perhaps the "Liberal Catholic" position that is most threatened by the conflict over homosexuality. The intensifying polarity surrounding the symbolic nature of the issue leads some occupying this location on the Anglican moral map to decide that justice toward gays and lesbians ought to be a normative principle that trumps other considerations, while others privilege the unity of the transnational church as being a more important principle to preserve. The difficulty that Rowan Williams appears to have in finding widespread support for any of his responses to the conflict supports our suggestion that this area of the map is finding the present storm difficult to weather.

To suggest that these are emerging divisions does not mean that they will be absolute, or that, in the end, they will necessarily be final. Much depends, in all likelihood, on the successful suturing of conservative Anglo-Catholics and conservative evangelicals into "Orthodox Anglicans." Furthermore, as additional research within the (now two) dioceses of Pittsburgh has revealed, to simply describe the conflict in simplistic terms as a battle between "liberals" and "conservatives" is problematic in other ways.

Schism in the Diocese of Pittsburgh

Of the four dioceses that have formally split from the Episcopal Church in the United States, the diocese of Pittsburgh is unique for two reasons. First, it is the only diocese of the four in which women can be ordained. Second, whereas the other three dioceses withdrew from TEC largely intact, the diocese of Pittsburgh split over the decision. Roughly two-thirds of the congregations in the diocese voted to withdraw from TEC, but one-third voted firmly to remain. This resulted in considerable pain and resentment on both sides, and many congregations were deeply divided internally.

The study in Pittsburgh to date includes fifty-four interviews, involving twenty-eight laypeople, twenty-five clergy, and one bishop. The study focuses primarily on five congregations, two of which remain in TEC, and three that have formally left and become part of the Anglican Church in North America (ACNA). As in the study of British bishops, the methodology employed primarily involves semistructured interviews, which ask participants to describe what happened in Pittsburgh, why their congregations made the decisions they did, and what they hope the future will bring for their church. The data from this study are still being analyzed, but some preliminary findings can be mentioned here.

The Breakdown of the Rhetoric of "Liberal" versus "Conservative"

There is a tendency, both within media treatments of the dispute with TEC, and also within the church itself, to describe the conflict as a clash between "liberals" (or often "progressives" in the U.S. context) and "conservatives" (or "evangelicals" in the Pittsburgh context). There is clearly some truth to this, but the ethnographic data challenge this dualism in significant ways.

A group of twelve clergy who self-identify as "conservative evangelicals" made public appeals against the decision to leave TEC, and when the split eventually occurred, they voted to remain in the Episcopal Church. One of them explains his position as follows:

> We are all Evangelical, and share some views with those who have "realigned" as they say, but we do not agree with breaking the dialogue. We want to see the process through. The Windsor process is ongoing, and we think it should continue and that we should be part of that.

In the course of the discussion, he laments about how he and his colleagues were treated by those who decided to join the ACNA: "We have been criticized, called traitors. It has gotten ugly."

Another member of the group of twelve recalls his own reaction to the emerging split:

> I found [it] to be really shocking because for years the bishop had said that he would never leave the Episcopal Church and that we would have to be kicked out, and yet here he announced that he had pretty much reversed that policy and that he was going to seek to take the diocese out of the Episcopal Church, and so I found that really shocking.

When asked to elaborate on his reasons for not leaving TEC, this "conservative evangelical" replied, "My understanding is the church is the body of Christ and you don't go around chopping it into pieces." He continued by adding that it is "pretty clear that division is not something that the New Testament countenances within the church, if you look at the passages as to what they actually say." This priest in a divided congregation concluded by remarking, "You know, frankly, during the tensions of the realignment a lot of self-righteousness began to be expressed, and I thought that was kind of a toxic thing for a Christian community."

Lack of Uniformity on the Issue of Homosexuality

If it is not difficult to find self-described "conservative evangelicals" who oppose the acceptance of gay clergy but still elect to remain within the "liberal" Episcopal Church, it is also noteworthy that it is not difficult to find members of congregations who have left TEC who are not at all convinced that homosexuality should be a primary issue of church division. One priest in a large and influential church in the ACNA diocese in Pittsburgh commented on this issue in the following manner:

> The big issue here [with realignment] is homosexuality. People always say that's not the issue, but that it's the gospel, it's the authority of Scripture, and that's true on one level. . . . But I'm not comfortable with the definition . . . of defining Christianity in terms of morals. . . . I feel like . . . the realigning creates a situation where we're known as kind of the homophobic church, the anti-gay church or whatever. There's already enough people out there looking for an excuse to not come to church and to reject religion.

Although uncomfortable with the consecration of Gene Robinson as a bishop, he also adds that "I had a number of conversations with friends from seminary who feel like this battle for the Anglican Communion is kind of our parents' battle. It's kind of a 'baby boomer' kind of thing." In his mind, making homosexuality the dividing line of the church is a poor witness to the wider society: "We grew up watching Will and Grace and all these crazy things. I mean, we've all known a lot of gay people and none of them have . . . They're not vampires!"

This tone was not uncommon among younger members (under thirty-five) of churches that had left TEC. One young woman, though concerned to emphasize that she thought that members of TEC disregarded the divine authority of Scripture, also asserted that the decision to leave the national church was a mistake:

> I don't think they [the ACNA congregations] should have just left them [the TEC congregations]. I think they should have stayed. . . . [We should have] stayed and helped them because, like, you've got children in your life [and you can't just abandon them]. We need to sort of point them back to what they believe in.

When asked about the issue of homosexuality, she said, "I confess I have a friend who is gay. . . . I don't agree with him, but I love him. And he's a Christian, and I know he's struggled with it, and the fact of that matter is, I have come to a place where I have to admit that I don't understand it." Although not prepared to say that homosexuality was not sinful, she also would not agree that it is any more sinful than a lot of other activities and practices that most people engaged in. More to the point, she thought it was a tragic mistake for her church to split over this issue.

The Prominent Role of Clergy

If there was one issue that laity and clergy in both TEC and the ACNA dioceses can agree on, it is that the position of the rector of a congregation determined how that community voted when it was asked whether or not they would leave TEC. When lay members were asked why the split had happened in Pittsburgh, in a congregation that remained within TEC, but in which many lay members openly declared disagreement with the ordination of homosexuals, one woman answered, "because the bishop [who called for realignment] was such a strong leader. People trusted him and so they followed him." But when asked why her congregation had not left, she credited the rector, who had argued that the church should remain in TEC. Another member of that congregation concurred, stating that the position of his priest "had everything to do with this church not realigning."

Members of other congregations made similar claims. This is not an insignificant observation. In a diocese that has become highly politicized and divided over issues of morality and theological authority, what appears to have been a key factor is determining whether a congregation removed itself from TEC or not was the leadership of the clergy in that congregation. It is this factor, rather than whether a congregation is "liberal" or "conservative," or how members view the ordination of practicing homosexuals, that is more influential for determining what direction a congregation went when the split in the diocese occurred.

Evidence of Pain and Lament over the Split

In much of the media coverage of the split within TEC, the opposing sides have been portrayed as monolithic in their positions on homosexuality, the authority of Scripture, and their "conservative" or "liberal" agenda. They have also been described as both loathing their opponents in the alternative diocese, and thus being relieved to be rid of them now that the split has occurred. This is not what my ethnographic data suggest. Many church members on both sides express considerable sadness over what happened to their diocese. Although few imagine that there is any hope for reconciliation or a coming together of the two dioceses in the future, many continue to mourn the division. In one congregation that is considered to be among the most "liberal" in the TEC diocese, the congregation prays publicly for clergy "who serve under other bishops" and mentions by name some of the ACNA priests now serving in the other Pittsburgh diocese. Although such a spirit may be less common among clergy in ACNA congregations, it is not difficult to find it among laypeople. The cathedral of the diocese is noteworthy for its refusal to formally align itself with either the TEC or ACNA diocese, but decided to offer itself as the cathedral of both groups. Such examples of resistance to the schism, or at least of continuing to pray for the other group, represent a fascinating glimpse of what "church" may mean to these individuals, and offer a great deal to ecclesiological reflection on the situation.

Ethnography's Contribution to Theology?

This small sample of observations made over the course of qualitative interviews and observer participation might be interesting, but do they make any significant contribution to ecclesiology? I argue that they do, and will conclude this chapter with three suggestions regarding the possibility that ecclesiology benefits from the sort of inquiry that ethnography represents. The first is a general point; the latter two relate to the particular content of my ethnographic fieldwork.

The Need for Reflexivity

John Milbank has perhaps advanced the most aggressive warning against the tendency of sociology to "police" a theological understanding of social, including ecclesial, life.[12] While it would be difficult to deny that this dynamic is possible (and often present), this risk should not be taken as support for the view that social-scientific attention to lived human existence *as such* is unhelpful to theology. Theological reflection and debate occur within a social space. Its reasoning and argumentation are conducted by fallible human beings. Ethnographic attention to the explicitly *nontheological* dynamics in which theology operates can only serve to help theology be more self-reflexive of its own activity. As the theologian seeks after God, it is surely helpful to attend to the very human and social limitations and frames that may shape this pursuit in overt but also subtle ways. Augustine writes in his *Confessions:* "To the best of my power and the best of my will I have laid this long account before you, because you first willed that I should confess to you."[13] In a context in which the church is tearing itself apart and facing schism, might not the act of stepping back from a focused attention on the disputed theological doctrines, in order to attend to those forces and dynamics that may be fueling the crisis, serve in some sense as an act of reflexive confession on the part of the theologian? If so, then there is a rather strong argument for suggesting that ethnography may serve an important role in ecclesiology. It contributes to the presentation before God of the church's present reality.

Mark Chapman observes that, although dogmatic theology is useful

---

12. Milbank, *Theology and Social Theory.*
13. Augustine, *The Confessions* (London: Penguin Books, 1961), p. 253 (Book XI.1).

for its analysis of sanctity, it may well be far from the best method for analyzing human sinfulness.[14] Attending to the context in which theology emerges, and in which it is received and employed as an aid to understanding, is an important component of theology's discipline and calling. To make this claim is not to suggest that ethnography is an unbiased or purely "objective" science that has a purer access to reality than does theology. Methodological reflection on the limits of ethnography highlights the need for the discipline's own self-reflexivity.[15] My argument is not that ethnography is somehow inherently less shaped by the worldview of the ethnographer than theology by theologian; it is simply that ecclesiology's self-reflexivity, as well as its capacity to attend to what is going on within the church, is enhanced by drawing from the disciplines of the social sciences. Contra Milbank, the debate between theology and social science need not be framed as two competing master narratives vying for domination, with one inevitably succumbing to the control of the other. If one discipline is described as being self-sufficient and unable to learn from another, then, I suggest, the scholar is being unwilling to be open enough to learn something new.

When initial recruitment appeals were being made for the congregational studies in Pittsburgh, invitations were often met initially with great suspicion and caution. The potential informants expressed the concern that the researcher's presence might make the internal tensions in their churches worse. They wondered whether my data could somehow end up involved in the ongoing lawsuits over property. They questioned my motives and my own theological agenda. In the end, the reason many accepted me in their midst was quite straightforward. As the priest of the most divided and damaged congregation that I visited said to me: "I would be very interested at the end of it all to read your insights, for sometimes it can be very difficult to have a clear perspective while immersed in something oneself." A prominent leader of a congregation phrased it this way: "Maybe you'll see something we don't."

Is there not a sense in which this attitude toward empirical research could be called "faith seeking understanding"? People caught up in the dispute within Anglicanism get tired of hearing the same story told about

---

14. Mark Chapman, "On Sociological Theology," *Journal for the History of Modern Theology* 15 (2008): 8.

15. See, for example, David Silverman, *Interpreting Qualitative Data*, 3rd ed. (London: Sage, 2006), pp. 377-97; Colin Robson, *Real World Research*, 2nd ed. (Oxford: Blackwell, 2002), pp. 455-99.

them over and over again. Ethnography offers the possibility that perhaps someone will notice something new, and such newness of insight will open doors for subsequent ecclesiological reflection.

The Limits of Normative Theology in a Climate of Theological Dispute

One thing that Anglican churches are not short of at present is confident doctrinal claims about the nature of the "true church." Much of this could possibly be dismissed as examples of careless or shallow engagements with the tradition, so that better systematic ecclesiology would rectify the situation considerably. Perhaps. However, in the face of the rhetorical violence of the existing state of affairs within these church disputes, straightforward dogmatic expositions on the nature of the church might only serve to add one further competing theological narrative to a context already wearied by and suspicious of such narratives. To make this point is not to call into question the value of dogmatic theology, but to raise the question of the practical and pastoral role of theology, and whether theology's task (and witness) is properly influenced by the audience to which it speaks.

It is at this point that sociological observation about the nature of symbols becomes a relevant and important resource for ecclesiology. When ecclesiological concepts like "inclusiveness," "orthodoxy," or even "Incarnation" and "Holiness" have become loaded with symbolic meaning, and mobilized in support of one ecclesial agenda in opposition to another, the theologian who intends to be of service to the church has little room to maneuver. This is further complicated when, as part of this tense atmosphere, individual people and groups are themselves turned into symbols: "Gay," "Conservative," "Liberal," "Homophobic," "Heretic," etc. As one priest in Pittsburgh diocese noted, "I started realizing that, wait a second, what I've been told [about other churches in the diocese] isn't necessarily true." He continued: "What I'd been told about St. Gonchar's and St. Malkin's, and what they think about God and Christ is not actually what they think and believe."

One option in response to this problem would be to work from different concepts in order to gradually modify any problematic ways that symbolic doctrines are being deployed. But another strategy is to begin by listening to those constructing the doctrines according to their agendas. In this way, the theologian can gauge the extent to which the primary symbols may only represent "presenting issues." Is the primary theological and ecclesiological problem necessarily the one that appears to present itself? Are the doctrinal materials that are being directly deployed in a given situation really the ones at stake in the dispute?

The attempt to bring ecclesiology and ethnography into closer relationship potentially serves this difficult process of discernment. What is theologically at stake in the present moment? While it requires grounding in tradition to adequately recognize the doctrinal resources at stake in ecclesiological study, and to appreciate how they relate to each other, the skills of ethnography are useful for being able to listen and attend to the presenting problems in order to begin to discern the situation or problem at hand.

The Capacity for Tensions within the Churches to Illuminate the Church

One of the clearest benefits of ethnographic research is in those moments when tensions or contradictions begin to come into view within the life of individuals or groups within the churches. The study of the particular does not necessarily suggest that the immediate thing that presents itself is considered the sum of reality. Rather, scrutinizing the particular can result in the recognition that what initially appears simple and straightforward is actually complex and mysterious. There is often an elusiveness to the object of study in ethnography, and this can be one of its principal contributions to ecclesiology.

When speaking with one longer-serving lay member in an ACNA congregation in Pittsburgh, I asked why she thought her church had to leave: "We couldn't stay in a sinful church! We had to take a stand! It was a choice between Christ and false belief." However, when asked what she thought about those who voted otherwise and had left her congregation, the tone of her voice, and the expression on her face, changed considerably: "I never imagined so many would leave! When they [the church leadership] saw what was happening, they should have stopped. It was too much! This wasn't right!"

The tension between these two positions — "We had to leave"; "We shouldn't have left" — is very interesting and illuminating. It is a brief glimpse into the complexity of an otherwise apparently simple and straightforward ideological dispute in the church. And this insight suggests that there is more going on here than is initially apparent. It is attention to such moments, rather than to the more direct doctrinal dispute that presents itself, that is a potentially fruitful place for theological ecclesiology.

Our ethnographic research on the Anglican Communion has illuminated many such examples: a parishioner speaking passionately about the stand her congregation has taken, then admitting that, as her church has become more militant, her faith has been waning; another lamenting over how many friends have left the church, leaving it without direction, but then speaking with pride and excitement over how formerly inactive people have now become highly involved in congregational life. The predominance of such examples in the life of the church illustrates that mere appearance is not simple reality. These are insights that offer much to the theological task of ecclesiology.

As it becomes clear that the speaking individual is not self-transparent, one observes how the church is not transparent to itself either. It emerges that the parts are not the whole. There is more going on than can initially be grasped. For the theologian, this might signal hidden ideologies, social forces, failures of reasoning, and so forth, but the theologian need not simply conclude this is all that might be at work. Such observations might also be, speaking theologically, signs of "moved movement."[16] The moments of tension, contradiction, or sheer mystery that emerge out of the thick descriptions of ethnographical study of church life are important contributions to ecclesiology. They do not reduce the church to indeterminate human acts, but actually complicate such a reductionist attitude. Rather than shutting out the search for the depth from which the church arises, they point beyond themselves and invite deeper reflection on new possibilities and interpretations.

During one interview with a senior church official, he lamented, "At the moment, the conflict [in the church] is shaping [us], and [the church] is not shaping the conflict." If this is true, then theological wrestling with the ecclesiological problem of church conflict requires that it begin to wrestle directly with how the conflict is shaping it. This is to say that there is a real sense in which the church's movement is being moved by something other than itself — but this may not be the work of the Holy Spirit. When the theological task is to work to discern what is indeed moving the church, the attentiveness to the lived reality of Christian communities represents a vital contribution to the task of ecclesiology.

Ethnography's capacity to contribute to an understanding of the

16. I borrow this expression from John Webster.

church's present life is not limited to a negative critique. The moments of tension and contradiction in ecclesial life may illuminate what ecclesiology could be more attentive to. If it is to "hear what the Spirit is saying to the Church," then such moments of interruption — the gaps in the present church's understanding of the limitations of its practices — highlight what may be important to rectify, avoid, speak to. While it will largely be the theological tradition that will provide the content to any description of the elusiveness of the reality being explored, Christian theology is here being tested and tentatively proposed, not only in dialogue with the past tradition of faith, but also the present life of the church. The theological concern against this (and rightly so) is to warn against taking the existing empirical church *as* the church itself, thereby losing any critical capacity for ecclesiology to call the churches into question. But I am not suggesting that ecclesiology simply take at face value what people in the churches say about themselves (negatively or positively), and no good ethnographer would assume that what people say is objectively true. What I am arguing, however, is that, exploring the tensions and contradictions that people themselves do not have a good handle on, or may not even recognize, offers promising insights and observations that contribute to theological inquiry. Just as theological doctrines might serve to interrupt and challenge the assumptions of the empirical church, the gaps and contradictions in the empirical church may refocus and call to attention certain issues for systematic theology.

The conflict over homosexuality in churches like the Anglican Communion brings into clear view that ecclesiology, if it is to help the church discern its true nature and calling, cannot remain at the level of ideal and abstract theorizing. The tensions and conflicts disrupting the life of contemporary Christian communities are too complicated and painful for the church to be transparent to itself, or to the theologian. It is here that the contribution of ethnography and other social-scientific methodologies to ecclesiology emerges. Without losing track of the proper goal and focus of ecclesiology, a disciplined exploration of the church's present reality can serve as an act of careful attentiveness to both the work of the Spirit and the challenges of human sinfulness, and also open up new paths of recognition of what the church is called to repent of, as well as to give thanks for. Ethnography does not reduce ecclesiology to contextual description; rather, it is through the "thick description" offered by ethnography that the theologian can begin to see past rhetorical language games and the political maneuvering that is such a part of church life, and begin to recognize that God's work in the church far surpasses our more limited expectations and agendas.

CHAPTER 7

On Discerning the Living Truth of the Church: Theological and Sociological Reflections on *Receptive Ecumenism and the Local Church*

Paul D. Murray and Mathew Guest

Introduction

In order to explore the relationship between ecclesiology and ethnography, this jointly authored contribution focuses on a particular collaborative research project in practical ecclesiology that is currently underway in the North East of England — *Receptive Ecumenism and the Local Church (RE&LC)* — which explicitly brings doctrinal, theological, and ethnographic sociological modes of analysis into close conversation in service, it is hoped, of the transformative study of the church. Hosted by the Centre for Catholic Studies within Durham University's Department of Theology and Religion and conducted over a four- to five-year period, *RE&LC* basically involves a mixed total research group of ecclesiologists, practical theologians, sociologists and anthropologists of religion, educational and organizational experts, local practitioners, and key church personnel working together to analyze the respective organizational cultures of nine of the major Christian denominational groupings in the North East of England with a view to asking how they might each fruitfully learn from the respective best practice of the other participant groupings.[1]

In the first part of the essay, Paul Murray, a systematic theologian and

1. The nine participant regional denominational groupings are: the Roman Catholic Diocese of Hexham and Newcastle; the Anglican Dioceses of Durham and Newcastle respectively; the Northern Synod of the United Reformed Church; the Methodist Districts of Darlington and Newcastle respectively; the Northern Baptist Association; the Northern Division of the Salvation Army; and the Assemblies of God.

the director of the project, introduces the thinking that drives *RE&LC* (A.1), its core aims (A.2), and its shape (A.3). In Part B Mathew Guest, a sociologist of religion and core project advisor to *RE&LC*, probes some pertinent sociological methodological issues before offering an original constructive proposal as to how these might best be conceptualized and approached relative to this project in terms of viewing it as an exercise in "collective ethnography." In the light of this sociological analysis, Paul Murray turns in the final section (Part C) to reflect on the specifically doctrinal ecclesiological significance of *RE&LC* both methodologically and substantively.

The main title of the essay, "On Discerning the Living Truth of the Church," is deliberately ambiguous, with intentional dual resonance indicating the range of commitments and concerns that are in play in seeking to bring theological and sociological perspectives on the church into constructive conversation. On the one hand it has scriptural and doctrinal resonance, recalling the Johannine language of "life," "truth," and "living water" used in reference to Jesus[2] — the one who is in turn regarded in Christian understanding as *the* living truth of the church, its founder, its impulse, the one to whom the church bears witness, the one whose mission the church's practices and structures should serve and reflect, and by whose Spirit it is believed these same practices and structures are themselves shaped. On the other hand it refers us to the living, breathing, "concrete" reality of the church as it actually is — or at least as ethnography might help us see how it is — and not simply as we would have it be or imagine it to be. Here we share Nicholas M. Healy's concern that

> In general, ecclesiology in our period has become highly systematic and theoretical, focused more upon discerning the right things to think about the church rather than orientated to the living, rather messy, confused and confusing body that the church actually is.[3]

We here offer the *RE&LC* regional comparative research project as a worked example of the kind of "practical-prophetic" alternative in

2. For Jesus as life and bestowing life, see John 1:4; 5:26; 6:33, 35, 48, 53, 57, 63; 10:10; 11:25-26; 14:6; 20:31. For Jesus as truth and the way of truth (and the Spirit as leading into truth), see John 1:14, 17; 8:32, 45-46; 14:6; 16:13; 18:37. For Jesus as giving "living water" and being "living bread," see respectively John 4:10-11; 7:38 (the last with explicit reference to the Spirit); and John 6:51.

3. Nicholas M. Healy, *Church, World, and the Christian Life: Practical-Prophetic Ecclesiology* (Cambridge: Cambridge University Press, 2000), p. 3.

ecclesiology for which Healy calls, one that seeks to engage seriously in the empirical study of the church as an integral dimension of a genuinely and robustly theological discerning of the living truth of the church.

Part A: The Anatomy of the Project and Its Theological and Methodological Presuppositions

A.1 *Seeking after the Living Truth of the Church: The Task of Ecclesiology in Postliberal Perspective*

Key theological, epistemological, and methodological principles at work in *RE&LC* — as also throughout the broader family of Receptive Ecumenism projects of which *RE&LC* is, to date, the most practically focused expression — have their origin in an earlier project exploring the appropriate character of theological reasoning in the light of the now widespread shift to postfoundationalist understandings of human knowledge, particularly as this shift is variously evidenced in the American pragmatist tradition.[4]

In essence we are dealing here with a dual shift, first *from* the image of knowledge as a superstructure progressively erected on the basis of sure and certain, discretely verifiable foundations and *to* the image of knowledge — particularly associated with Willard van Orman Quine — as a complex, flexible, context-specific web.[5] Second, we are dealing with the shift *from* viewing truth purely in terms of cognitive understanding and linguistic and conceptual articulation alone *to* recognizing the need to

4. For the first major text emanating from the Receptive Ecumenism projects, see Paul D. Murray, ed., *Receptive Ecumenism and the Call to Catholic Learning: Exploring a Way for Contemporary Ecumenism,* with foreword by Walter Cardinal Kasper (Oxford: Oxford University Press, 2008), particularly Murray's preface, pp. ix-xv, and chapter 1, "Receptive Ecumenism and Catholic Learning — Establishing the Agenda," pp. 5-25; also Murray, "Receptive Ecumenism and Ecclesial Learning: Receiving Gifts for Our Needs," *Louvain Studies* 33 (2008): 30-45. For the earlier project focused on postfoundationalist theological reasoning, see Murray, *Reason, Truth, and Theology in Pragmatist Perspective* (Leuven: Peeters, 2004). For something of the relationship between these projects, see Murray, "On Valuing Truth in Practice: Rome's Postmodern Challenge," *International Journal of Systematic Theology* 8 (2006): 163-83; also Murray, "Receptive Ecumenism and Catholic Learning — Establishing the Agenda," in *Receptive Ecumenism,* pp. 7-8.

5. See Willard van Orman Quine, "Two Dogmas of Empiricism" (1951), reprinted in Quine, *From a Logical Point of View: Nine Logico-Philosophical Essays,* 2nd ed. (Cambridge, MA: Harvard University Press, 1980), pp. 20-46, particularly pp. 42-43. For comment, see Murray, *Reason, Truth, and Theology in Pragmatist Perspective,* pp. 35-40.

view truth also in performative terms of efficacy and fruitfulness, and this not just as a means of testing for cognitive truth but as part of what truth actually is.[6] In this way of understanding, truth is not simply about seeking to recognize and articulate the reality of things but also about discerning and living in accordance with the fruitful possibilities that the open-textured reality of things presents. In scriptural terms, "Not every one who says to me 'Lord, Lord,' shall enter the kingdom of heaven, but he who does the will of my Father who is in heaven."[7]

Taken together, this dual shift represents the relinquishing of rationality as an aspiration for watertight cognitive security and absolute certainty built around linear modes of reinforcing progression and the contrary embrace of an understanding of rationality as a never-ending, recursively expansive process of situated, self-correcting scrutiny in service of: (1) sound understanding of what is and what might be; (2) reasoned evaluation of the most appropriate way forward; and (3) effective practical implementation of same.[8] Here the aspiration for "objectivity" is understood not in terms of an unattainable neutrality and delusional desire for a "view from nowhere" that seeks to bracket out context and perspective but, following Donald Davidson, in terms of a process of triangulation and mutual accountability.[9] Such ideas recur later in the novel category of "collective ethnography," proposed as an appropriate way of configuring the processes of understanding and accountability in *RE&LC*.

In theological terms, the above-outlined presuppositions feed into and serve to fill out an expanded postliberal theological commitment that

6. See Murray, *Reason, Truth, and Theology in Pragmatist Perspective*, pp. 7, 62-63, 64-68, 75-77, 119.

7. Matt. 7:21/Luke 6:46-49. See also Matt. 19:17/Mark 10:17-19/Luke 18:18-20; Mark 3:35/Matt. 12:50/Luke 8:21; Mark 4:20/Matt. 13:23/Luke 8:15; Luke 11:28; John 14:21; 15:14.

8. See Murray, *Reason, Truth, and Theology in Pragmatist Perspective*, pp. 91-130, particularly pp. 93-123.

9. For the phrase "the view from nowhere," see Thomas Nagel's book of that title (Oxford: Oxford University Press, 1986). For Donald Davidson on objectivity as triangulation, see "Rational Animals," in *Actions and Events*, ed. Ernest LePore and Brian McLaughlin (Oxford: Blackwell, 1985), pp. 473-81 (p. 480); also Davidson, "A Coherence Theory of Truth and Knowledge" (1983), reprinted with "Afterthoughts" in *Reading Rorty: Critical Responses to Philosophy and the Mirror of Nature (and Beyond)*, ed. Alan Malachowski (Oxford: Blackwell, 1990), pp. 120-38 (pp. 120-21, 123); and "On the Very Idea of a Conceptual Scheme" (1974), reprinted in Davidson, *Inquiries into Truth and Interpretation* (Oxford: Clarendon Press, 1984), pp. 183-98 (p. 198). For comment, see Murray, *Reason, Truth, and Theology in Pragmatist Perspective*, pp. 40-49, particularly pp. 45-48.

takes seriously the need to start out from the particularity of Christian tradition and the consequent theological inappropriateness of taking any other discipline (whether philosophy, law, social theory, ethnography, the natural sciences, or whatever) as systematically foundational for Christian theology, while also wanting to guard against the notes of triumphalism, completeness, sufficiency, and superiority that can too easily infect the postliberal theological stance.[10] Contrary to any such potential postliberal complacency, the argument at work here is that the core commitments and dynamics of Christian tradition themselves require — particularly so when read in conjunction with the postfoundationalist account of human rationality traced here — both a due emphasis on Christian particularity and for this to be held open to a continual, even if ad hoc, process of scrutiny and self-critical accountability relative to a range of other perspectives and disciplines in turn regarded as having their own integrity.[11] As a means of holding together a similar constellation of concerns, Rowan Williams suggests the language of "celebratory," "communicative," and "critical" to speak of three necessarily interacting "styles" and interwoven responsibilities in Christian theology: while theology rightly begins in celebratory rootedness in the particularities of Christian faith, if it is not to risk becoming "sealed in on itself" it needs both to engage in "fruitful," potentially mutually enlightening "conversation" with the "rhetoric of its uncommitted environment" and to pursue with rigor critical questions concerning the meaning, coherence, and adequacy of received articulations and performances of Christian tradition.[12]

10. For theological postliberalism, the seminal text is George A. Lindbeck, *The Nature of Doctrine: Religion and Theology in a Postliberal Age* (London: SPCK, 1984). For comment on Lindbeck and expansion of the principles briefly noted here, see Murray, *Reason, Truth, and Theology in Pragmatist Perspective*, pp. 11-16.

11. See Murray, *Reason, Truth, and Theology in Pragmatist Perspective*, pp. 131-61, particularly pp. 152-61; also Murray, "A Liberal Helping of Postliberalism Please," in *The Future of Liberal Theology*, ed. Mark Chapman (Aldershot, UK: Ashgate, 2001), pp. 208-18. As the reference to this process of expansive, self-critical scrutinizing being "ad hoc" and relative to other disciplines and perspectives regarded as having their "own integrity" might indicate, the expanded postliberal account articulated here is entirely commensurate with that also in view in Nicholas Healy's essay in the same volume.

12. See Rowan Williams, prologue, in Williams, *On Christian Theology* (Oxford: Blackwell, 2000), pp. xii-xvi. I am grateful to Paul Lakeland for reminding me of Williams's usage here. The work of Nicholas Lash could also be appealed to at this point as also demonstrating a similar constellation of concerns and self-critical, expansive postliberal theological persuasion; see n. 21.

There are a number of ways in which the above-outlined understanding of theological rationality and approach feed directly into *RE&LC*.

First, the nine participant regional denominational groupings are accordingly treated as complex webs of thought and practice, the understanding of which requires a multi-perspectival approach drawing, as appropriate, on a broad range of analytical approaches beyond the traditionally theological in order to facilitate this.

Second, the aim is not simply to understand and describe these various webs but to identify areas of difficulty, tension, incoherence, awkwardness, even dysfunction, with a view to exploring how they might each potentially be rewoven in order to address their respective difficulties. This is to view the task of ecclesiology as a form of diagnostic, therapeutic analysis; as a means of address and repair for systemic ills; as an agent of change.

Third, as this implies, these webs of thought and practice are regarded not simply as providing the context within which the ecclesial reasoning of the respective participant groupings occurs but as actually embodying this reasoning.[13] The point is that real theological reasoning is embodied in the way, for example, in which Christian communities make decisions and not simply in the arguments that are given in support of the rationality of particular beliefs. It is in relation to such matters as discernment — both practical and doctrinal — and the exercise of authority that the rubber of theological reasoning hits the road of church life. If we wish to ask whether, in practice, a particular Christian tradition or denominational grouping reflects the kind of dynamic, expansive, self-critical reasoning that was earlier advocated, it is to such matters that we must look.

Fourth, this in turn implies the need to examine the extent to which differing webs of ecclesial reasoning, differing webs of thought and practice, are capable in practice of learning from each other. It is here that the ecumenical — and specifically the receptively ecumenical — dimension of the project comes in. Here ecumenical encounter is viewed not simply as posing a series of seemingly intractable problems for the Christian churches but as opening a field of opportunities in which a potential process of expansive, self-critical learning from the alternative ecclesial experiments of other traditions could occur that would resonate powerfully with the earlier outlined understanding of sound ecclesial reasoning. Given its centrality to the *RE&LC* project, it will be helpful now to explore the

---

13. See Elaine Graham, *Transforming Practice: Pastoral Theology in an Age of Uncertainty* (London and New York: Mowbray, 1996), p. 90.

thinking behind Receptive Ecumenism and the earlier related projects in a little more detail.

A.2 Receptive Ecumenism: Core Principles and Aims

Receptive Ecumenism is a strategy devised to respond to the contemporary ecumenical context. Clear recognition is given to two apparently opposed points: (1) that for a number of reasons the hope for full structural and sacramental unity as a realizable goal that drove much classical ecumenical work has receded from view as a realistic proximate aspiration; (2) that the ultimate goal of full structural and sacramental unity — however that might variously be imagined as being configured — must nevertheless form an essential and abiding orientation for Christian ecumenism as a non-negotiable gospel imperative.[14] Poised in this manner between current and foreseeable non-realization on the one hand and the imperative non-negotiability of the fundamental orientation on the other, the fundamental ecumenical need for the Christian churches in this context is to find an appropriately imaginative way of living this orientation in the here and now; of walking now the way of conversion toward more visible structural and sacramental unity in the future.

Accordingly, at the heart of Receptive Ecumenism is the basic conviction that further ecumenical progress will indeed be possible but only if denominational traditions make a shift from typically asking what other traditions might fruitfully learn from them and instead take the creative step of rigorously exploring what they themselves might fruitfully learn (or "receive") with integrity from their "others." This represents something of a JFK-style reversal: "Ask not what your ecumenical others must learn from you; ask rather what you must learn from your ecumenical others." If all were acting on this principle — indeed, even if only some were acting on this principle — then change would happen on many fronts, albeit somewhat unpredictably.

Much ecumenism is about, as it were, getting the best china out; about wanting others to see us in our best possible light. In contrast, Re-

---

14. For more on this and on what follows, see Murray, "Receptive Ecumenism and Catholic Learning — Establishing the Agenda," in *Reason, Truth, and Theology in Pragmatist Perspective;* and "Receptive Ecumenism and Ecclesial Learning: Receiving Gifts According to Our Needs," also in *Reason, Truth, and Theology in Pragmatist Perspective.*

ceptive Ecumenism is an ecumenism of the wounded hands, of showing our wounds to each other, recognizing that we cannot save ourselves but trusting that we can be ministered to by each other, receiving in our needs from each other's particular gifts.

As has been noted on a number of occasions and reflecting the theologically worked pragmatist principles guiding them, each of the initial projects in Receptive Ecumenism were concerned not simply to theorize about the church and to engage in purely doctrinal reimagining alone but to seek to diagnose and address experienced problems with the actual lived structures, systems, cultures, and practices of the church.[15] The basic principle here was that the church is not primarily a doctrine, a theory, but a living, breathing life-world. Almost inevitably, however, the various analyses that were pursued in the first two projects, even when practically oriented, nevertheless tended to operate at a relatively abstract, theorized level. This showed the need for a further, much more practically focused project that would examine the relevance, viability, and on-the-ground implications of Receptive Ecumenism at the level of local church life; with "local church" understood as embracing both the regional level of diocese, district, synod, or equivalent and the more immediate level of parish or congregation, together with the intermediate level of deanery, circuit, or equivalent.

The idea was born of a major collaborative comparative research project involving as many of the Christian denominational groupings in the North East of England as possible, in partnership with staff of Durham University's Department of Theology and Religion (both theologians and sociologists/anthropologists of religion), Durham Business School (organizational, human resource, and financial experts), St. John's College (practical theologians), the North of England Institute for Christian Education (NEICE), and the various regional ecumenical officers and other local church practitioners. The purpose would be to examine how respective specific difficulties in the organizational cultures of each of the participant denominational groupings — and the doctrinal theological commitments associated with these — might fruitfully be addressed by learning from/re-

---

15. The two initial projects were focused on international research conferences: the first, in January 2006, tested the strategy in relation to potential Catholic receptive learning, exploring also how the various practical, cultural, psychological, and organizational hindrances might be mitigated (see n. 4 here); the second, in January 2009, extended the strategy to all other Christian traditions and will be published as *Receptive Ecumenism and Ecclesial Learning: Learning to Be Church Together*.

ceiving of examples of "best practice" in the other traditions. As such, the idea was to use practical and organizational matters — and the social-scientific means of analyzing these — as rigorous yet ultimately ad hoc means of testing, checking, and expanding the explicitly theological.

A.3 Receptive Ecumenism and the Local Church: The Shape of the Project

The need was rapidly identified for three related yet distinct trajectories of research, each with its own research team working in a coordinated yet relatively distinct fashion and focusing respectively on *Governance and Finance; Leadership and Ministry;* and *Learning and Formation.* Each team, with total membership of about eight in each case, is led by a professorial-level expert with significant expertise in an extratheological discipline: *Governance and Finance* by a professor of business ethics of Durham Business School; *Leadership and Ministry* by a professor of human relations, also of Durham Business School; and *Learning and Formation* by a professor of Christian education of the North of England Institute for Christian Education.

Whereas the *Governance and Finance* team is directly concerned with the organizational cultures and systems of authority, accountability, strategic planning, and finance that are operative in each of the participant denominational groupings,[16] *Leadership and Ministry* is concerned with how these are administered and shaped by the respective cultures and practices of leadership. In turn, *Learning and Formation* asks how the respective cultures and identities of the churches are nurtured, transmitted, shaped, and challenged through the habits, practices, experiences, structures, and strategies pertaining to learning and formation that are operative — either explicitly and deliberately or implicitly and accidentally — at various levels.

It is possible to think in terms of there being five broad phases to the project. For each team, the first task was to conduct an initial, detailed mapping of what is currently happening, at least in theory, in each of the participant denominational groupings, and the formal theological self-

---

16. The work of the *Governance and Finance* team, although developed entirely independently and operating on a far, far smaller scale, bears some comparison with the significant work of the National Leadership Roundtable in the U.S., focused on promoting better management and financial practices in the U.S. Catholic Church; see http://theleadership roundtable.org/.

understanding that pertains in each case. These mapping exercises were carried out on the basis of available documentation (e.g., authoritative theological self-descriptions, mission statements, terms of reference of relevant committees and bodies, minutes, etc.) cross-referenced with a select number of informal interviews aimed at facilitating interpreter comprehension. The initial reports that derived from these Phase I mapping exercises were offered back to key representatives within the respective denominational groupings for them to consider and comment upon.

Following this, the aim of the second main phase of work was to begin to move from the Phase I level of theory and principle to the relevant lived reality and actual practice in each of the traditions. The threefold purpose was: (1) to test how the respective theories work in practice; (2) to begin to identify respective areas of good practice and difficulty/dysfunction alike; and (3) to begin to identify where fruitful receptive learning might potentially take place across the traditions, whereby one tradition's particular difficulties might be tended to, or enabled, by another's particular gifts.

To these ends each research team engaged upon a discrete broad-based empirical data-gathering exercise utilizing a range of approaches from the more directly quantitative in the case of *Leadership and Ministry* (questionnaire) to the more qualitative in the cases respectively of *Governance and Finance* (structured interviews with key/representative individuals in each denominational grouping and at each of the relevant levels of region, congregation, and intermediate structure) and *Learning and Formation* (group listening exercises/focus groups and participant-observer analysis). Further, while each of these data-gathering exercises was primarily focused on the specific interests of the particular research team in question, they were each also explicitly alert to the concerns of the other two teams and so able, using different methods and research groups, to gather some additional relevant data for the purposes of the other groups. As such, the aim was to build in a degree of triangulation not only within the work of the respective teams but also between them.

In turn, the third key phase of activity — underway at time of writing — is seeking to extend considerably the dimension of triangulation that was already a feature of Phase II by pursuing two time-limited ethnographic congregational studies in each denominational grouping that are explicitly intended to bring the three core concerns of the research teams into integrated focus. To this end, these Phase III cross-trajectory studies are focused on the common issue of the challenges presented by the declining numbers of full-time ordained/authorized ministers and the respective strategies being adopted by the participant denominational groupings to respond to these challenges. Here we have an issue that brings into common focus matters pertaining to governance, decision-making, finance, leadership, and formation. The interim reports deriving from these case studies will be shared, in each case, with the congregations that shared in the studies.

Following the completion of the data-gathering stages of *RE&LC* (Phases I, II, and III), the fourth phase will focus on analyzing the data in the round and seeking to identify on this basis the respective gifts (examples of good practice) and needs (areas of difficulty/dysfunction) in each denominational grouping. This in turn should allow some cogent and specific proposals to be made concerning ways in which the needs of one grouping might fruitfully be addressed by learning from something of the gifts of the others. Clearly it will not be enough here simply to indicate such possibilities in a vague, hypothetical manner. Each proposal will need testing through in terms of: (1) the degree to which it can be shown to cohere with relevant core doctrinal convictions in the overall web of the host grouping and, correlatively, the degree to which the overall web can be legitimately reconfigured, even rewoven, in order to accommodate the proposal in question; (2) its practicality (e.g., its financial, organizational, and cultural costs); and (3) its ability to attract support within the proposed receiving denominational grouping. As such, this process of testing through will need to be carried out in close conversation both with the relevant formal, authoritatively articulated theologies and actually operative theologies (as disclosed in Phases II and III here), as also with key subgroups within the groupings. The point will be to identify all possible objections and to examine whether a reasonable way forward can be found. Those proposals that survive this iterative process will be regarded as robust and worthy of serious consideration. It will be these that are offered to the respective denominational groupings.

The final phase will be that of dissemination. This will operate at a number of levels. Most immediately — and, perhaps, most important — it will consist in the production of a distinct report for each participating denominational grouping, containing a number of well-thought-through and tested practical proposals for real potential receptive learning within that regional grouping, proposals that hold the promise of enabling each grouping to live their respective callings and mission more fruitfully. Alongside and reinforcing these reports, it is hoped that more directly practical and face-to-face dissemination will take place in the region through the reports being discussed, together with key team members, by all the appropriate committees and decision-making bodies within each participant grouping and at the three relevant levels of region, congregation, and intermediate structure. There will in addition be a further major academic volume providing a thorough methodological and theological analysis of the project and of the constructive doctrinal ecclesiological work that will figure in the testing and refinement of the project's proposals. Finally, there will also be a series of popular-level publications aimed at widely promoting the basic strategy of Receptive Ecumenism including, most notably, a set of resource materials that Churches Together in England have committed to producing for local groups wishing to pursue the path of receptive ecumenical learning.

Part B: Toward a Collective Ecclesial Ethnography: Sociological Perspectives on *Receptive Ecumenism and the Local Church*

RE&LC aims to bring the various participating denominational groupings into, to borrow a phrase from Don Browning, "mutually critical dialogue."[17] While a pressing issue, this aspiration is by no means an original one. What makes this project distinctive is its determination to ground this dialogue in empirical research. The various parties involved will, it is hoped, engage in a critical and reflexive process of self-examination and mutual learning, basing their self-knowledge not merely on established doctrinal traditions, but on what they discover about themselves using empirical research. This central task is no mean feat, and raises a whole host of questions about the nature of this kind of ecclesiological exercise. Not least, it is worth emphasizing that just because ethnography[18] is working in the service of theological questions, this does not mean it is any less subject to the methodological challenges surrounding its deployment

---

17. See Don Browning, *A Fundamental Practical Theology* (Minneapolis: Fortress Press, 1991).

18. Ethnography is taken here as the description of a cultural phenomenon (literally, "writing culture"), and involving the extended study of a human group in their "natural" context, drawing on a variety of — chiefly qualitative — research methods. For discussions of the definition of ethnography, see Martin Hammersley, *What's Wrong with Ethnography? Methodological Explorations* (London: Routledge, 1992); and Perti Alasuutari, *Researching Culture: Qualitative Methods and Cultural Studies* (London: Sage, 1995).

within the social sciences. Issues of validity, representativeness, the ethical responsibility of the researcher, the politics of subjectivity, professional loyalties versus loyalties forged "in the field," the power relations embedded in the writing process — all have their place in discussions among theologians about how they properly and most effectively handle empirical research as a source of knowledge. We should note that this is not, in our view, a one-way street. The social sciences, in their own deployment of ethnography, also have much to learn from their colleagues in theology, not least on account of a more pervasive and developed engagement among theologians with epistemological debates focused on questions of truth and the status of truth claims (see A.1 here). While there has been much fruitful discussion among social scientists on this issue — one might note Charlotte Aull Davies's grounding of a reflexive ethnography in Roy Bhaskar's vision of critical realism[19] — there remains much to do, and more fruitful debates will ensue if theology and social science enter more deeply into conversation as distinct but engaged disciplines rather than building insurmountable boundaries around themselves.

To return to the challenges facing *RE&LC*, one stands out as particularly difficult, raising crucial avenues of debate pertinent to the theological appropriation of social-scientific method, and concerning the aspiration to generate normative claims on the basis of empirical investigation. The project assumes the desirability and legitimacy of questioning the status quo. This raises numerous tricky questions: Who has the right to offer critique, and how do they earn it? How does one balance the professional obligations one has as an ethnographer to the academy with the moral obligations one has to those who are the subjects of the study, bearing in mind that these subjects may also be members of one's own church? What place is to be given to critical voices that might emerge from each domain but which clash with one another, presenting a challenge to the coherent cultural portrait sometimes expected, and indeed hoped for, by the industrious participant observer? Moreover, might there be circumstances in which a clear, coherent, and well-bounded portrait of Christian life in a particular locality might not be a desirable, responsible, or illuminating aspiration? Here we might consider Frances Ward's ethnographic study of a mixed-race congregation in Manchester, which draws from poststructural theory in advocating an ethnographic discourse that fore-

19. See Charlotte Aull Davies, *Reflexive Ethnography: A Guide to Researching Selves and Others* (London: Routledge, 1999).

grounds fragmentation, disruption, and difference as a precondition for identifying and facilitating a voice for the otherwise marginalized members of a church, in this case, its black members.[20]

What we propose to do in this section is take two interlinked challenges and offer a brief engagement with each from a sociological perspective. Our hope is that by attempting to grapple with methodological, conceptual, and epistemological challenges presented by an ongoing empirical research project, we will foster discussion that might shed some real light on the interdisciplinary dialogue between ethnography and ecclesiology. Our focus will be on two connected challenges, which may be addressed via a consideration of cognate debates in the social sciences. Both have analogues among social scientists in general and among social scientists engaged with theological concerns in particular. Both have to do with issues of method, although the first has a more epistemological relevance while the second raises more in the way of ethical issues. We will reflect on (1) how we might discern and describe the identity of a particular church, and then, in light of this, (2) how the tensions between descriptive and normative accounts might be ethically and effectively negotiated. A final section will discuss how each of these issues might be addressed through the adoption of an approach we are calling "collective ethnography."

B.1 Ethnographies of "Church"

While the empirical study of the Christian church — whether via national surveys, or on a more local or institutional level — now has a fairly lengthy history that has produced numerous rich published accounts, few of these have engaged seriously with the question of the social construction of Christian community.[21] It has been taken on board by many theologians and sociologists that the church needs to be acknowledged as a concrete, material, embodied, and human phenomenon, fashioned by the fires of history and social upheaval like any other institutional entity. It is also recognized that we would do well to examine the social life of the church us-

---

20. Frances Ward, "The Messiness of Studying Congregations," in *Congregational Studies in the UK: Christianity in a Post-Christian Context,* ed. M. Guest, K. Tusting, and L. Woodhead (Aldershot, UK: Ashgate, 2004).

21. Notable exceptions are: Peter Stromberg, *Symbols of Community: The Cultural System of a Swedish Church* (Tucson: University of Arizona Press, 1986); and Al Dowie, *Interpreting Culture in a Scottish Congregation* (New York: Lang, 2002).

ing the tried and tested tools of sociology and anthropology. However, how we get from the empirical data at our disposal to the description of church life we offer as the conclusion of our study is a question less often faced. Assuming an eclectic toolbox of research methods — as is often the case in such studies — how do we take a collection of written observations, interview transcripts, church records, notes on informal conversations, questionnaire responses, and a healthy dose of intuition born of personal experience, and transform it into a coherent and meaningful account of church life? The assumption that this transformation might be straightforward or unproblematic is absurd as much as it is disturbing. For an uncritical methodological strategy that fails to address this issue can only compromise a research endeavor: at best throwing into question the epistemological standing of its claims, at worst papering over power inequalities or acts of misrepresentation that have more serious ethical implications.[22]

RE&LC faces this daunting problem on a number of levels. First, at the level of personnel, the project involves a large number of researchers, analysts, advisors, and stakeholders, not to mention those responsible for directing the project. Within the context of such collaborative research, goals of coordinating data collection and analysis so as to facilitate a convergence of insights and the construction of a fair and illuminating picture are all the more challenging. Second, our analysis of church life among the various denominations in the North East rightly distinguishes between different levels of organization and governance: the local, intermediate, and regional. The multiple voices one might expect to encounter within a study of churches as singular phenomena might therefore be multiplied three times over, and as the higher echelons of power enter into consideration, so the various discourses in evidence start to gather more force and may be expected to carry more impetus in their ambitions to dominate and influence the research agenda, an issue to which we will return later.

Third, there is, as in arguably all social groups, a distinction to be drawn between what Gerd Baumann has called "dominant" and "demotic" discourses.[23] In this context, we might speak of "official" versus "popular"

22. These challenges are perhaps most visible within the writing processes involved in ethnography, as it is here that aspects and voices are "edited out" as the "final" picture of a social collective is formalized. See John van Maanen, *Tales of the Field: On Writing Ethnography* (Chicago: University of Chicago Press, 1988).

23. Gerd Baumann, *Contesting Culture: Discourses of Identity in Multi-Ethnic London* (Cambridge, New York, and Melbourne: Cambridge University Press, 1996).

perspectives, the former enshrined in constitutional documents and embodied in church leaders, the latter constructed at the grassroots level, among ordinary churchgoers, whose outlook on various issues might be quite different from their vicar's, priest's, or minister's. An advantage of an ethnographic approach, with its longitudinal dimension and attention to subtlety and detail, is that it allows some investigation into how these different discourses have come to take their present form. One does not have to look far for some excellent published studies that have pursued this line of approach with illuminating results. In the U.S., we might turn to R. S. Warner's exemplary ethnographic study of a small-town Presbyterian church, *New Wine in Old Wineskins*, which engages the lived reality of church life among leaders and townsfolk. What is produced is a rich account of change: from liberal to evangelical sympathies, as filtered through the experiences of ordinary churchgoers and the ministers subject to their shifting allegiances.[24] Closer to home, Tim Jenkins's *Religion in English Everyday Life* includes a study of the village of Comberton near Cambridge, offering an evocative picture of contemporary rural parish life. What is striking here is how perceptions of the local church, its significance, legitimacy, role, and purpose, are radically shaped not by doctrinal allegiances, but by embedded understandings of village identity and the social-class structures endemic to it.[25] At the very least, ethnographies of Christian churches need to consider how a multitude of discourses constitute congregational life.

Fourth, life within the various church communities involved in this project is inevitably colored not just by perceptions and experiences of life in St. Peter's, the West Durham deanery, in the Durham diocese, to take a fictional example, but by a perceived participation in more abstract collective entities, such as Christianity, or, at the level of churchmanship, for example, the evangelical, Anglo-Catholic, or charismatic movements. Such subtle affiliations may be best described, following Benedict Anderson's work, as "imagined communities,"[26] collective and supralocal entities that are constructed and maintained by their members in dialogue with inher-

24. R. S. Warner, *New Wine in Old Wineskins: Evangelicals and Liberals in a Small-Town Church* (Berkeley, Los Angeles, and London: University of California Press, 1988).

25. Timothy Jenkins, *Religion in English Everyday Life* (New York and Oxford: Berghahn Books, 1999). See also Martin Stringer, *Contemporary Western Ethnography and the Definition of Religion* (London: Continuum, 2008).

26. Benedict Anderson, *Imagined Communities: Reflections on the Origin and Spread of Nationalism* (London: Verso, 1991).

ited traditions and ongoing efforts at self-identification, via ritual markers and sometimes collective disputes. These differing shades of British Christianity have been with us for a long time, some for centuries, but they are worth mentioning here because recent controversies over Christian identity, priestly authority, and moral teaching have engendered a new, organized level of affiliation, one that has for some arguably overtaken the local congregation as the primary point of identification for grassroots Christians in Britain. The widespread — sometimes divisive — influence of organizations like Forward in Faith, the Fellowship of Confessing Anglicans, and Reform are testament to this, and at the very least indicate a stratum of engagement that, in accordance with debates at local, regional, and national levels, may often generate a reconfiguration of loyalties among churchgoers. With such lines of affiliation and protest cross-cutting local expressions of denominational, regional, and generational identity, it is unsurprising that the task of capturing the identities of local churches is an elusive one.

B.2 Descriptive and Normative Accounts

Aside from the issue of constructing, appropriating, or assembling some kind of descriptive account of identity from the fragmented pieces of congregational life, the challenge of producing a coherent account brings with it other problems of a political nature. In recent decades, social scientists have subjected the history of ethnography to deconstruction and postcolonial critique. Notable here was James Clifford and George Marcus's 1986 volume, *Writing Culture: The Poetics and Politics of Ethnography*,[27] which collected together a series of essays critiquing the assumed objectivity and unproblematic knowledge claims of classical anthropology. The work of the founding fathers of participant observation, such as Bronislaw Malinowski and Raymond Firth, as well as more recent authors like Clifford Geertz, is examined in light of postmodern and postcolonial theory, the authors unmasking how the cultural and academic identities of these "masters" were constitutive in their construction of the ethnographic "other." A value-neutral ethnography was, so it seemed, impossible, and at the very least, authors ought to exercise critical reflexivity in offering de-

---

27. James Clifford and George E. Marcus, eds., *Writing Culture: The Poetics and Politics of Ethnography* (Berkeley, Los Angeles, and London: University of California Press, 1986).

tailed and transparent reflections on how their own cultural baggage finds its way into their analyses. The long-term impact of Clifford and Marcus upon the social sciences has proved to be variable: some ignore their work in favor of a traditional, realist approach which, so they claim, retains legitimacy, with at best a perfunctory reflection on the construction of key concepts. Others have taken fully on board their critique of ethnographic writing, to the point where their newly conceived "postmodern ethnography" no longer constitutes an attempt to represent a social reality "out there," for all that truly exists is the self-emanating discourse of the ethnographer as a cultural agent caught in the assumptions, language, and categories of his or her own situated identity.[28]

These are extremes. At the very least, the debate surrounding Clifford and Marcus's book alerts us to the danger of assuming a straightforward and clear-cut distinction between descriptive and normative accounts. No ethnographies emerge "from nowhere"; all are a product of a particular — or several — individual(s), located within a particular cultural and academic context, the result of a particular set of questions being asked in a particular way of a particular community at a particular time. If the context of the community under study is historically situated, so is the context of the ethnographer conducting the study. These constraints are inescapable, and the question of how they are negotiated through practical research strategies and epistemological discussion is not easily resolved. Many acknowledge their situatedness as authors, and then write their ethnographies with no further reference to this observation. Others go back to something approaching first principles in deconstructing key concepts and rebuilding them from scratch, and yet remain themselves virtually invisible within the emerging written account.[29] One approach is simply to acknowledge the implicitly normative nature of research, render this explicit, and put it to work in the service of a particular agenda. While this may sound attractive — and familiar — to theologians seeking to put empirical study in the service of particular ecclesiological or doctrinal arguments, it has been most systematically formulated among social scientists. To take one example, Paul Willis was known in the 1970s as a pioneer of cultural studies, and for conducting a

28. A striking example can be found in Sarah Caldwell's ethnography of a Kali cult in India; see Sarah Caldwell, *Oh Terrifying Mother: Sexuality, Violence and Worship of the Goddess Kali* (Oxford and New Delhi: Oxford University Press, 1999).

29. This may be said of Tim Jenkins's ethnographic study of English religion. See Jenkins, *Religion in English Everyday Life*.

series of ethnographic studies among working-class men and members of youth subcultures. What distinguishes Willis's work is his explicitly Marxist perspective, which shapes both his motivation for study and his understanding of his task as a sociologist. Writing in 1977, in his influential study *Learning to Labour: How Working Class Kids Get Working Class Jobs*, Willis notes:

> The role of ethnography is to show the cultural viewpoint of the oppressed, their "hidden" knowledges and resistances as well as the basis on which their entrapping "decisions" are taken in some sense of liberty, but which nevertheless help to produce "structure." This is, in part, the project of showing the capacities of the working class to generate, albeit ambiguous, complex and often ironic, collective and cultural forms of knowledge not reducible to the bourgeois forms — and the importance of this as one of the bases for political change.[30]

Willis's vision of ethnography is instructive in several respects. Not least, it offers a methodological strategy for offering the marginalized a new voice, a place within a discourse, a role in a collective identity within which they were previously hidden and oppressed. While there may be some space for a theological critique of Willis's Marxist assumptions — both substantively as social critique and methodologically as a questionable basis for study — his approach nevertheless demonstrates how an external agenda can be put to work via ethnographic study. Moreover, in challenging existing dominant discourses, Willis opens up space for change and reform, aspirations at the heart of *RE&LC*. It is worth expressing this more technically, as it is highly important to the vision of a collective ethnography that follows. What we are advocating is an explicit but discriminate attempt to relativize the social reality within churches among those within them, or at least among those who lead them. By relativizing what might be taken to be fixed traditions or conventions, and exposing their contingency upon specific socio-historical conditions, ethnographic analysis might open up the possibility of positive change among the communities under study. Insofar as *RE&LC* has as one of its key aims the enablement of church leaders to discern aspects of their denominational "culture" that might be improved or enhanced in light of lessons learned from others, this decoupling of churches from established conventions might be a precondition of its suc-

30. Paul Willis, *Learning to Labour: How Working Class Kids Get Working Class Jobs* (Farnborough, UK: Saxon House, 1977), p. 203.

cess, for only if change is considered to be possible can change be entertained as a practical and theological ambition.

B.3 Proposing a "Collective Ethnography"

In this way, ethnographic study itself may enable conversations conducive to receptive ecumenism, but only if roles within the research context (researcher, practitioner, leader, etc.) are effectively managed, and if these churches effectively share the ownership of the ethnographic study. In this sense, this kind of ethnography may be said to be potentially emancipatory, and we would argue that this is both a desirable and important outcome because a precondition of change is the freeing up of church members and leaders from the presumed inevitability of embedded conventions. To encourage change we first have to recognize that things need not be as they are.

However, ethnography may only be emancipatory if there is an effective separation of leadership structures and the ethnographic voice, with each thereby operating within a mutually critical — perhaps prophetic — relationship. Practicalities stand in the way of this ideal model in this context because those church members most available, able, and willing to act in the role of ethnographer are also in many cases their priests or ministers. Of course, these individuals are arguably best placed to do this, on account of their prior knowledge and position within local church networks. The obvious danger, however, would be that existing leaders rehearse and re-embed the community structures that they themselves embody, and in so doing produce an only partial account of their church's life. Or, their account is taken to be authoritative by church members because of their status.

To address this, we are proposing here a model we are calling "collective ethnography," with practitioners empowered by the academic (and ecclesiastical) community to be ethnographers of their own churches and to build a picture of themselves via conversations enhanced by engagement with others in their church, and with those in other churches, hence facilitating an ongoing dialogue with multiple nodes of activity. This model avoids the danger of standardization and homogenization, our first challenge, by elevating the status of all ethnographic voices to an equal level, each holding the other to account, and reflecting Elaine Graham's call for pastoral theology to genuinely begin with the experiences of Christian communities, in all their internal diversity and situatedness.[31] It also addresses the issue of normativity by obliging transparency on the part of all involved and issuing emerging findings in a more subjunctive, rather than imperative, voice. It draws from Paul Willis's model of ethnography in focusing on the empowerment of lost voices (including here lost aspects, features, and traditions), not as a means primarily to alleviate oppression, but to facilitate a more authentic and multifaceted account of church life. In this way, this approach presents a means of negotiating the problems of leaders studying their own churches, as they are held to account by other ethnographers and by the project group as a whole, quite aside from the channels of feedback and conversation that would be opened between project researchers and representatives of their churches and denominations. In building essentially on channels of conversation, this model sets up the communicative and epistemological means of generating the kind of exchange that is central to *RE&LC*. What it does not do is identify how such lines of conversation might achieve agreement or closure, although whether that is a desirable prescription at all is perhaps a moot point.

Part C: The Doctrinal Theological Significance of Practical Ecclesiology and Ecclesial Ethnography

Prior to exploring the basic vision and strategy of Receptive Ecumenism (A.2) and the specific shape of the current regional comparative research project in *Receptive Ecumenism and the Local Church* (A.3), the first section of this essay started out by identifying and reflecting on various of the key theological, epistemological, and methodological principles that have specifically informed the conceiving of the ecclesiological task at issue in the Receptive Ecumenism projects (A.1). Having now engaged with the practicalities of *RE&LC* and considered how the social sciences may contribute to the resourcing of this project (Part B), it is appropriate to return to explicit consideration of methodological matters in ecclesiology as these pertain to *RE&LC*.

Here the basic question is as to what exactly is the doctrinal theological significance of such an exercise in the empirical study of the church, or ecclesial ethnography. Alternatively posed, in what sense is this kind of practical ecclesiology a genuinely ecclesiological exercise? What does it

---

31. Graham, *Transforming Practice*, p. 93.

contribute to the systematic, doctrinal, ecclesiological task? Does empirical study of the church simply serve to illustrate the characteristic denominational practices and cultures associated with respective formally articulated ecclesiologies? Or does it have some more directly critical, constructive, and genuinely theological contribution to make to the systematic, doctrinal, ecclesiological task? And perhaps prior even to these questions: In what sense is it genuinely theologically appropriate — and not simply practically expedient — to incorporate a methodologically naturalist discipline, such as ethnographic sociology necessarily is, as a necessary turn or moment into an authentic understanding of the Christian theological task? Reflections here in relation to these questions will be ordered in two steps: (1) a few words in qualified general support for a necessary naturalist moment in Christian theology; (2) a few words more specifically on the necessary role of empirical sociological (and other) studies in doctrinal ecclesiological testing for the living truth of the church in practice.

C.1 The Intrinsic Need for a Certain Naturalist Moment in Christian Theology

To approach this issue we can profitably reflect briefly on the responses Thomas Aquinas gives to two articles, or subsequent questions, he poses in his *Summa Theologiae,* the first of which, at first sight at least, appears to take us in anything but a naturalist direction. These are *ST* 1a.1.7, concerning the subject of Christian theology, and *ST* 1a.47.1, concerning the multiplicity and distinction of things as deriving from God.

Having established that Christian theology can properly be regarded as a science (*ST* 1a.1.2, also 1a.1.3-6), Aquinas turns in the seventh article under the first question on "what sort of teaching Christian theology is and what it covers" to ask "Is God the subject of this science?" His response, famously, is that as the very word *theology,* or "talk about God," suggests the subject of theology is indeed God — while recognizing that God is not a thing of any kind — but also of all particular things in relation to God as their source, sustainer, and consummation.[32] As such, the-

---

32. See Thomas Aquinas, *Summa Theologiae,* vol. 1, *Christian Theology (1a.1),* ed. Thomas Gilby (London: Eyre & Spottiswoode; New York: McGraw-Hill, 1963), 1a.1.7, pp. 25-27, particularly: "Now all things are dealt with in holy teaching in terms of God, either because they are God himself or because they are relative to him as their origin and end" (p. 27).

ology rightly has a perspective on everything. It is about understanding all things in relation to their originating and ultimate, rather than merely proximate, orientation: in relation, as it were, to God as first and final cause, and not simply in relation to the realm of secondary causes to which more methodologically naturalist disciplines confine their attention. Indeed, the clear implication is that things are not understood fully or aright until they are understood in theological perspective.

At first sight, this theological "queening" over the sciences does not appear to hold out much prospect of a positive regard for the contribution of a certain naturalist moment in theological understanding. If it is only in theological perspective that a full account of any particular thing can be given, what real contribution is made by naturalist perspectives that can at best, it would seem, be considered partial and provisional?

An answer to this question is implicit in Aquinas's response to the first article under question 47 on the plurality of things.[33] Posing the question as to whether "the multiplicity and distinction of things is from God," Aquinas replies in two stages. First, he reminds us that God's purpose in creating anything at all is so that God's "goodness might be communicated to creatures and reenacted through them." Second, he notes that being finite, any creature can only communicate God's goodness partially and inadequately. Hence, it is necessary for there to be an abundant diversity of things ("many and diverse") so that "what was wanting in one expression of divine goodness might be supplied by another" and, thereby, the abundant goodness of God be figured forth more adequately. As Aquinas puts it: "Hence the whole universe less incompletely than one alone shares and represents his [God's] goodness."

This gives us deeper perspective on what it means to think of theology as a process not just of understanding God but of all things in relation to God as their source, sustainer, and consummation. This is not simply about completing our knowledge of things by bringing them into explicit relation with the only finally adequate perspective within which to understand them. It is every bit as much about the deepening and enriching of our theological understanding through asking after the myriad particular ways in which something of the goodness of God is shown in and through finite, created reality — albeit always in partial and disfigured form — and what it means to live before and within the gift of God in these circum-

---

33. *Summa Theologiae*, vol. 8, *Creation, Variety, and Evil (1a.44-49)*, ed. Thomas Gilby (London: Eyre & Spottiswoode; New York: McGraw-Hill, 1967), 1a.47.1, pp. 91-97.

stances (who in God's-self remains unknowable).[34] This in turn implies that far from the concern to view things in naturalist perspective necessarily being a confusing, even corrupting, distraction from more properly viewing them in theological perspective, such a naturalist viewing is in fact — or at least can be when properly pursued — a necessary moment in a genuinely theological understanding of things.

The point is that if we are to understand how a mineral, or a plant, or an animal, or a human social life-form, or the fundamental physical laws of the universe manifest, each in its particularity, something of the goodness of God and what it means to live in accordance with this, then it is necessary to take time to understand each such finite reality in its own right, with all its own immensely complex particularity in view. It is here that we require, even for ultimate theological purposes, the services of the focused perspectives of the methodologically naturalist disciplines. While our prior starting point might appropriately be with explicitly theological convictions concerning, for example, all things having their origin, being, and end in the trinitarian life of God (or concerning the church being the Spirit-indwelt people of God), and while we might appropriately intend to end up asking how the given area of finite, created reality in question — whether the laws of physics or an aspect of the life of the church — is to be read in explicitly theological perspective, our actual understanding of these finite created realities in all their complex particularity requires other frames of analysis than the explicitly theological alone. Indeed, not to take account of what can be understood of a given area of finite created reality from within the perspectives of the focused naturalist disciplines will lead not to a purity of appropriate theological understanding but to its confusion and occlusion. The same is true whether the area of finite created reality in question be the fundamental laws of physics, the com-

34. For St. Thomas, while "holy teaching" (his term for theology conducted in the light of God's self-revelation rather than purely in terms of what can be known of God on the basis of natural human reasoning alone) is primarily a theoretical rather than practical science ("it is mainly concerned with the divine things which are, rather than with things men do"), it is never a matter of theoretical knowledge of God for its own sake but always in service of helping us understand how most appropriately to live well before and within the gift of God in the circumstances of this life. It is, we might say, a matter of theoretical analysis and knowledge — a theoretical science — in service of practical wisdom. See *Summa Theologiae*, vol. 8, 1a.1.2, 4, 6, pp. 17 and 21-25 in particular. For God in God's-self as remaining always unknowable in this learning of "holy teaching," see 1a.1.7, p. 27 and *passim*.

plex realities of human sexuality, or the living, breathing reality of the church.[35]

C.2 The Role of Empirical Accountability in Testing for the Living Truth of the Church

Bringing the general remarks above about the need for an appropriately naturalist moment in theological understanding to specifically ecclesiological focus, we might say that part of the ecclesiological methodological significance of the *RE&LC* project is that it is seeking precisely to avoid moving too quickly from appropriate prior theological convictions about the church and reflection on these to detailed claims about the church's supposed reality and associated practical implications without attending patiently to what is seen of the actual reality of the church when viewed in empirical sociological perspective. By integrating this empirical "moment" or "turn" within *RE&LC,* the aim is to escape the tendency, identified by Nicholas Healy, of pursuing ecclesiology in an abstract, purely theoretical-conceptual mode that operates in an ideal realm detached from the concrete reality of church life. But this alone does not exhaust the aims and desired ecclesiological significance (both methodological and substantive) of *RE&LC.*

Vital though it is to the ecclesiological task to seek to gain as full and accurate depiction of the actual reality of church life as possible and for the articulation of ecclesiology to be held in real conversation with this, and vital though the role of empirical sociology and other disciplines be in gaining such a depiction, this does not yet get to the core aim of *RE&LC.* The point is that *RE&LC* aims not simply to give better, more accurate depictions of the church but to perform a critical-transformative role; to contribute to the reconfiguring of the respective ecclesial webs of the participant regional groupings. Alongside, in Williams's terms, "celebration" and "communication," at the heart of the assumed role of Christian theology in *RE&LC* is that it is a process of "critical reflection on Christian practice" — we might add also "constructive reflection" — with a view to

35. Insofar as the argument here is in support of the real and necessary contribution that is always required by a certain naturalist moment, or turn, within the overall process of a robustly Christian theology, it is to be clearly distinguished from any attempts at a thoroughgoing theological naturalism such as that attempted by Willem B. Drees in his *Religion, Science and Naturalism,* 2nd ed. (Cambridge: Cambridge University Press, 1998 [1996]).

diagnosing its ills, whether conceptual, historical, hermeneutical, or practical, and enhancing the quality of this practice.[36] That is, the aim is to test for and search out that which, in theological terms, signifies grace and that which is culturally, organizationally, and practically discordant, even dysfunctional. Having done this, the further aim is to ask how the relevant ecclesial webs might be rewoven with dynamic integrity so as to ameliorate, even overcome, that which is dysfunctional by learning/receiving from that which tangibly bears grace in the respective others. As such, the relationship between the more explicitly ecclesiological concerns of *RE&LC* and the extended use of empirical sociological methods that are integral to it is — from the ecclesiological perspective — not simply one of extended and refined description but one of critical accountability.

It is well recognized that the more traditional theological partner disciplines of philosophical, historical, linguistic, and literary-textual — and, more recently, natural scientific — analyses are capable of performing not just as vehicles for the fresh articulation of otherwise substantively unrevised established convictions and doctrinal tenets but as significant means for the testing and, where necessary, revising of such convictions and tenets.[37] This process of critical accountability might be thought of as operating at the dual levels of *internal coherence* — "Can the convictions and tenets in question be articulated in such a way as enables them to hang together without tension and contradiction?" — and *extensive coherence* — "Can the convictions and tenets in question be articulated in such a way as enables them to hang together with what we otherwise have good reason for understanding about relevant aspects of the world?"

So also, the various approaches and methods of empirical sociology

---

36. On the role of Christian theology as one of critical-constructive reflection on Christian practice, see Nicholas Lash, *A Matter of Hope: A Theologian's Reflections on the Thought of Karl Marx* (London: Darton, Longman & Todd, 1981), pp. 208 and 133; and Lash, "Doing Theology on Dover Beach," in *Theology on Dover Beach* (London: Darton, Longman & Todd, 1979), pp. 3-23 (p. 14); Lash, "Ideology, Metaphor and Analogy," in *Theology on the Way to Emmaus* (London: SCM, 1986), pp. 95-119 (pp. 101, 103); "Theory, Theology and Ideology," in *Theology on the Way to Emmaus*, pp. 120-38 (p. 137); "Criticism or Construction? The Task of the Theologian," in *Theology on the Way to Emmaus*, pp. 3-17. For comment and analysis, see Murray, "Theology 'Under the Lash': Theology as Idolatry Critique in the Work of Nicholas Lash," *New Blackfriars* 88 (2007): 4-24, reprinted in *Idolatry: False Worship in the Bible, Early Judaism and Christianity*, ed. Stephen C. Barton (London: T. & T. Clark, 2007), pp. 246-66.

37. See Lash, "Ideology, Metaphor and Analogy," in *Theology on the Way to Emmaus*, pp. 103-5; "Theory, Theology and Ideology," in *Theology on the Way to Emmaus*, p. 138.

(as also any other cognate disciplines) may rightly be regarded in the ecclesiological context as being similarly capable of performing not simply as means of extended and refined description but as means of critical testing. Where for other typical theological partner disciplines (e.g., the natural sciences, philosophy, etc.) this process of critical accountability may most commonly operate at what have here been identified as the levels of *internal* and *extensive* coherence, in the case of the social sciences it may more appropriately be regarded as generally operating at the level of *pragmatic coherence*. By this I mean that it could be thought of as operating, in the first instance, at the level of the relationships that pertain between a given theological conviction or doctrinal tenet on the one hand and the actual habits, practices, values, structures, systems, and interpersonal relationships that these same convictions and tenets allow to happen, even promote, whether intentionally or unintentionally, on the other hand.

In short, what are the practical consequences that follow from, or are supported by — whether unintentionally, tacitly, or explicitly — a particular theological conviction or doctrinal tenet, and how do these consequences disclose weaknesses in the convictions and tenets themselves and suggest the need for them to be rewoven in order to counter these weaknesses? The key principle here is that if a way of thinking consistently and recurrently promotes, or serves to legitimate, an undesirable practical consequence, then it raises questions about the adequacy of the way of thinking itself and the need for it to be revised.

Of course, this in turn raises the need for a return to explicitly theological modes of analysis wherein the relevant webs of practice and belief are carefully assessed with a view to establishing whether or not they can be reconfigured, even expanded, with integrity in order to accommodate — to "receive" — the identified aspect of desired potential learning. In short, the prolonged exercises in ad hoc engagement with the social sciences — the empirical "moments" or "turns" — that are in view in this understanding of the ecclesiological task not only start out from explicitly theological and doctrinally laden contexts but properly return there for discernment as to their theological adequacy.

CHAPTER 8

God at Street Level: Digging Up the Theological Identity of Pastoral Care among the Homeless and Drug Addicts

Henk de Roest

A pastor says, and I quote:[1]

> She brings up a present that she had gotten from me and had given to someone else because she considered it a good thing to do so. It was a little cross that she had asked for earlier, while adding that she did not believe. And then, all of a sudden, right when we are about to say goodbye, she says, "Can you give me ten Euro?" "No," I say, slightly surprised. And while looking at each other she continues, "You should say: No, bitch!" We burst into laughter. Then there is silence. "What do you have for me?" she asks. "Nothing at this moment," I say, but I add: "A blessing." (I have not done or said anything like this to her, because of a time she told me that she does not believe in "God or in any commandment." "Ah, yes, yes, that is something you have to say," she says with a sigh, laughing again. Hesitating at first, I take her hands in mine and, with the blessing of St. Patrick at a distance, I say: "If there is a Spirit, if there is someone, a Present Being, a God, Someone who sees us, let it be here, and let it be with you, going before you as a Light, a Perspective, let it be above you as a protecting Hand on your head, under your feet as a solid ground, behind your back as support, beside you as you are yourself a fellow neighbor to others. So be it." She hugs me. We thank each other, she for the conversation and I for the reprimand.

1. Cf. Bernadette van Dijk 2010.

This kind of encounter demands a common withdrawal to a safe place, in order to continue one's journey. This kind of moment does not bear sharp publicity, but asks to be guarded. We hear biblical language and there are no general phrases about the divine, but the pastor names God who surrounds a vulnerable human being, gives support, and indicates direction. The pastor does not speak *about* God but speaks out of a connection with the God who expresses himself in Scripture.

* * *

Whoever raises theological questions in the area of pastoral care with drug addicts and the homeless[2] will be confronted with stories and anecdotes that are being told by pastors. Four years ago, the Dutch national network of street pastors identified the need to explore these stories in order to come to a thorough theological reflection.[3] Theological reflection was considered necessary because this kind of pastoral care is inseparable from the person of the pastor. Furthermore, replacing someone is difficult; new

2. Some data on the homeless and drug addicts: In 2002, one-third of homeless people (35 percent) were defined as "risk-drinkers," that is, they drank more than twenty-five glasses a week; 23 percent drank more than fifty-six glasses a week; and 13 percent more than 112 glasses a week (Bruin, Meijerman, Verbraeck 2003). In 2002, 52 percent of homeless people were cannabis users, and 47 percent had "consumed cocaine in the month before the inquiry." In 2006 in Rotterdam, 29 percent of the homeless population used cocaine on a daily basis. Many drug addicts are homeless. Recent data demonstrate that the number of homeless people is now estimated to be 56,000 (Voortgangsrapportage maatschappelijke zorg, Ministerie VWS April 2009, 18, table 2). The number is decreasing due to better housing facilities. Their situation is very complicated. Survival is the basic concern. Trust in other people is low. Contacts with relatives are often difficult. Mental and bodily problems dominate existence. Often there is also a difficult relationship with organizations that offer help and guidance (Davelaar et al. 2006).

3. Drugs and Street Pastoral Care came into being in the late 1970s, closely connected to pop-in centers. In 1977 in Groningen the first pop-in center was created. The Open House of the Paul-Church in Rotterdam opened its doors in 1980. Pastoral care for and with drug addicts started in Amsterdam in 1990. The Voice in the City in Haarlem began in 1995. Street pastors started working in Amsterdam in 2003. In my hometown, Amersfoort, a street pastor began her work as late as 2007. An article in the Dutch nationwide newspaper *Trouw* asserts: "The street pastor is advancing" (*Trouw,* 2 January 2004). This type of pastoral care and its accompanying community formation are made possible by local churches, diaconal institutions, and foundations. In Holland, street pastors are working in Amsterdam (also drug pastors), Arnhem, Delft, Den Bosch, Amersfoort, Rotterdam, The Hague, Groningen, Haarlem, Leeuwarden, Nijmegen, and Utrecht. Volunteers are assisting in all kinds of practical work (cooking, cleaning, administrative work, etc.).

pastors need a long time to adapt. In addition, it was hoped that such theological reflection might be helpful in other arenas as well. Twenty street pastors who are working in the main cities of the Netherlands took part in several meetings in which questions were asked like these: Is there common imagery in the rich stories street pastors tell? Can these images and metaphors be embedded theologically? What are the "theological foundations" on which this type of pastoral care is grounded?

At a meeting in May 2008, the pastors were asked to bring a symbol with them, to engage in conversation about these symbols and the values they convey:

> "As a pastor you walk alongside people on their journey." *(symbol: a backpack)*
>
> "You receive a lot in return from the people." *(symbol: a drawing of a hand)*
>
> "You get in touch with the real, pure, and sharp sides of people." *(symbol: a stone)*
>
> "You want to touch people who are touched by no one, people who are in a way untouchable." *(symbol: a drawing of a finger)*
>
> "I hope to offer an opportunity for reflection and friendship." *(symbol: a resonance bowl)*
>
> "Pastoral care on the streets hopes to offer people an oasis." *(symbol: a leaf)*
>
> "We hope to create a safe place, where people can feel at home." *(symbol: a pastry mold)*

The pastors concluded that working with these symbols proved helpful to reflect upon the *proprium* of their work. During the meeting, core values emerged such as: offering a free space, faithfulness, patience, openness, connectivity through solidarity with the people one works with, and reciprocity. In addition, something happened during the meeting that was initially not expected. Because the participants came to such a strong consensus that God can and may be brought to the foreground in these open engagements, they expressed a desire to share their work with others during their next meeting.

In January 2009, another meeting was held with all twenty pastors participating and five of the pastors offering presentations, each responding to different questions. Three outside theologians joined the meeting to reflect alongside them. Insights that were gained during the discussion were recorded, and, though it was not a focus group, I took my own field notes in order to dig up and excavate a *theological identity*. What emerged was a *theology of affirmation*. The pastors demonstrated an attitude of attentiveness, and they shared a particular anthropological view: homeless people could be viewed as God's image-bearers. It is the dignity of the homeless that is at stake, and it is this dignity that the pastors seek to protect and enforce. Finally, the theology of these pastors is interwoven with their God-talk and their spirituality.

In my inquiry, it struck me that three questions of identity were all closely related: (1) Who are we as pastors? (2) Who do we want to be as pastors? And (3) What kind of pastors should we be? On the one hand, the identity of the pastor becomes visible in her actual practice: what actions she chooses, what symbols she uses, how she is attentive, how she creates space to tell a life story, how she communicates her anthropological view, etc. On the other hand, her identity has a normative component. What she demonstrates is determined by the kind of pastor she believes she ought to be. Personal background is a variable in that, but also education and one's learning experiences within the field. Norms and values have been shaped theologically, but they may also be derived from other traditions or contexts. One can observe that a meaningful, recognizable presence is not detached from an ambition to be present in a meaningful and recognizable way. There is an ideal that is operative here, a calling that introduces a tension toward one's actual behavior. From the perspective of the homeless people, they have specific expectations that are based upon implicit and explicit promises the pastors make. Both the pastor and the homeless use idealized criteria to judge the acts of the pastor. For example, "'Ah, yes, yes, that is something you have to say,' she says with a sigh, laughing again." The pastor uses these criteria, too, as in, "I have not done or said anything like this to her, because she once told me that she does not believe in 'God nor in any commandment.'" So, when we speak about identity, there is always an intricate relationship between reality and an ideal, factuality and validity. This is true for the individual identity of the pastor, but also for the common identity of the professionals together if there are common characteristics.

In the five presentations that I observed, the pastors, although hesitant, nevertheless spoke about God in a candid, frank way. In their work, at times they act on behalf of God. Furthermore, they notice and respond to the implicit and explicit references to God that are made by their conversation partners. Faith language is present in abundance. The pastors long to express their hope; they want to listen to the longings and the free, audacious theological reflections of the homeless. They seek to facilitate real dialogue in which there is space for voice and dissent. They listen but they also are sure to express a promise. They make full use of their theological knowledge and skills. They are using a hermeneutical competence, by which they make the "transcending meaning of the story both hearable and expressible" (Ganzevoort 2001).[4] God is brought to the fore, but always in connection with the story of the other. What makes the other desperate? What gives him or her hope?

In the discussions with the pastors and stories they shared, there was a modest, yet unreserved and remarkable reliance on the Bible. For example, this showed up in the conversations with the homeless, in rituals, and in a story of a monument erected on the grave of someone deceased. Each conversation gives an opportunity to discover the meaning of biblical stories. For the theological identity of street pastors, Scripture plays an important role. They have the stories, parables, and images at hand, so to speak. We sense in the descriptions of their work that pastors try to find words and images of hope in these situations.

In the five descriptions I observe five elements. First, we see how the pastors *view* the people they work with in a theological way and how this view marks their actions. Second, we see how the *intentions* of the pastors shape their actions. They want to be present and they want to intervene. Apparently, that is also expected from them. They enter each scene with a metaphorical clerical collar. The people know that the pastors "have something with God," as they put it. Third, there is a *receptive* attitude, and they feel a strong obligation to have this attitude. Fourth, the pastors strive for *reciprocity*. Fifth, there is a focus upon establishing *relationships* and enabling people to tell their stories. Time and again, the pastors themselves tell about short conversations that took place in encounters which in turn become situated in a relational context. Relationships are being constructed, and within these relationships stories are told, words spoken, and rituals performed. In what follows, I elaborate these five characteristics.

Views about God and Man

> *"We do not do what others can do better in the form of treatment or facilities with regard to bed, bath, and bread. . . . We want to be*

4. Cf. Ganzevoort 2007, 120.

someone . . . someone who listens, someone who has an eye for the other, someone who accepts him or her at that moment and someone who respects his or her value, respects his and her silences."

"No one is lost in God's eye."

"When he left I shook his hands. The only thing that I could say was: 'We believe in you. I sincerely hope you will also believe in yourself.' Then he relaxed."

"I want to see the human being behind his pain."

Street pastors are eager to communicate their anthropological view. They have a strong mission to communicate it, too. This homeless person, no matter his or her condition, is in God's eyes a valuable, precious human being. This unique person bears God's image. She is not identified by her problematic situation, and she has a story to tell. She comes from somewhere and goes somewhere. She needs a space in which there is safety and she needs someone to be a witness of her life. She needs someone who accepts her, even though she is addicted and uprooted. She needs someone who believes in her and someone who reminds her that one's life can change. I would call it a *theology of affirmation*. Respectfully, the pastors sit beside them, where others do not wish to do so. They see their grandeur and their misery and see that the homeless long for warmth, love, and kindness. Finally, the pastors connect this with God's loving care for people and the way Jesus included people precisely because they are valuable.

Intentionality

"In every encounter, every meeting I go into, it is with the conviction that God is there at that moment."

"Each moment can become a moment in which we experience God, a moment when we recognize in each other's faces the face of God."

"I want to show them God's endless love."

"I want to give a bloom, a light to the life of a human being."

"A boy once told me that he feared that his soul was dead. This is terrible. I began to tell him about the Rose of Jericho. . . . 'Perhaps it is the same with your soul,' I said. 'Perhaps,' he said."

Second, in the descriptions they give of their work, we see a longing for relationship building. Often there is only a single encounter, but the pastors hope that they will at least get a name and hopefully they will get to hear their stories. They strive for meaningful relationships and a first contact that might lead to additional contacts. In these relationships there is an attentive openness for an "epiphanic moment." The pastors have an intense longing to communicate something from God. The encounter and its relational context may call for a "kerygmatic moment," ascribing a gift or quality to the other. While guiding people and accompanying them, a *new perspective* can be opened. The pastors have a longing to connect this with the mission of God and to characterize the addicts, for example, as "confused Emmaus travelers." They also seek an opportunity to communicate a whisper, in which a parable or biblical story can be told.

To be more nuanced, the intentional structure of the pastors has a *double* character. On the one hand, their approach is marked, colored by what Baart has labeled the "presence-approach" (Baart 2001). Attentiveness, being there, mutual recognition, unconditional acceptance, being open for surprises, and being approachable are all important. The pastors desire to get in tune with the lived life of the other. On the other hand, the pastor makes himself knowable too. Problem solving is bracketed because it is the relationships that count. The other has to be offered time to tell about himself, but as a pastor you may also show yourself, as we have seen in the story of the St. Patrick blessing. It is attentiveness in itself that may excite wonder and the offering of patience and time that is salutary. When trust is created, the other knows that he or she can feel safe with the pastor. In these instances, vulnerability and failure are not considered a reason to discontinue the relationship. It is precisely the people of the street — whether addicted or not — who are experiencing a society that would rather not see them. For the pastors themselves to experience these people of the street as seen, valued, and esteemed and then to know that their care for others is noticed and so the street people, too, want to know them is also salutary. "Well done," the pastor says encouragingly as she affirms with empathy. With their laughter, a certain lightheartedness is also present in the encounter. It is what in the presence-approach is called *thinned seriousness* — the relating to weighty themes in the midst of everyday acts like walking, setting the table, doing the dishes, or shopping together. It makes what is serious and heavy bearable.

Furthermore, these pastors not only intentionally locate the nearness of God in these encounters, but they name it or even proclaim it. These pastors look for life-giving images — like the Rose of Jericho — that can encourage and give hope. At times, a pastoral countervoice can be necessary, precisely because someone's life is going downhill. In the pastors' descriptive moments in which this happened, it is striking. In these encounters in which one listens to silences, the sight of God can be opened (Bons-Storm 1989, 21). The imagination of the pastor is very important. This is the heart of theology here. When we speak of these moments as sacred ground, mystical moment, spiritual moment, or Sabbath moment, there is an operative force in the words, leading to clarification and change.

Receptivity

"If anywhere, God is in the people that I meet."

"I am deeply moved and inspired if a man who has quit drinking a while ago, and is trying to get work experience again, tells me that he visits his brother — an alcoholic — weekly on Wednesdays while he is in jail. He embodies that he is his brother's keeper. A meeting like this sheds a light upon my day."

Again and again I saw how pastors do not only want to listen but also want to learn from the homeless, and how they are inspired by them. One pastor told of being surprised by hearing "Silent Night" played on a mouth-organ and experienced it as a gift. Another told how fascinating it is when people tell about a connection they have with a biblical story and what it means to them. Usually, they have appropriated the story in their own specific, unique way. She learns from these free interpretations. These pastors are intrigued by the hermeneutical creativity of their conversation partners. A receptivity can also be observed in the pastors' willingness to be challenged to or ask new questions. They wonder where the other is behind the veil and they want to receive their hope and despair.

Reciprocity?

The ideal and experience of reciprocity permeates the pastors' descriptions. One pastor wrote that she hopes the other will recognize something of God's face in her, but she hopes to see something of God's face in the other as well. The pastor, with whom I started this session, wrote that she learns from the lives, wisdom, and love of her conversation partners. She wrote that she is dependent on the welcome of the other.

Naming this reciprocity also serves to safeguard and protect the integrity of the agenda. What do you want from me? Do you want to bring me something or can I give you something, too? Do you want to help me and should I be grateful, or can I be there for you, too? Do you have a hidden agenda? Being transparent is essential.

Furthermore, the relationship between these pastors and their conversation partners should not carry the burden of reciprocity or mutuality. There are clear differences that turn the relationship into an asymmetrical one. The pastor, for example, remains responsible for guarding the boundaries of the encounter. As a professional, he or she also knows that it is the well-being of the other that matters, and not the needs of the pastor. In addition, his or her intentions are of a different order than the intentions of the conversation partner. Finally, the pastor herself is living in a different situation. Not only does she go home after a day's work, but she also goes to training, makes inquiries, improves her skills, reflects upon her attitude, learns from colleagues and from her mistakes. She has leisure time and other everyday activities. Having said this, it is striking to see how the pastors wish to articulate what is being offered to them. This should not be troubled by the ideal of reciprocity.

Connections and Community Formation

> *"Passing through the valley of weeping, they make it*
>   *a place of springs.*
> *Yes, the autumn rain covers it with blessings. We want to*
>   *create a place of springs . . ."*

Making connections and building up relationships also leads to community formation. Bringing people together, that is where ecclesiogenesis begins, even if this community has a very loose and flexible character. There is communitas around a funeral ceremony, for instance, where pastors are attentive to imaginary family members who come up in conversation or in prayers. These pastors know the importance of sociability, particularly after a church service, and how there is space in this time for questions about faith. It is about belonging without conditions. Is it a way of being church? Take note, the pastors warn us: these people do not want to be annexed. And yet, in the self-descriptions, I do sense that they consider themselves to be a form of church. Indeed, in the words of the drug addicts of Amsterdam: "This is our church."

Finally

We have outlined the contours of a theological identity of street pastors. I did not have the contributions of the homeless themselves, yet it seems their impressions of the pastors coincide with the pastors' descriptions. In their observations, the pastors "have something with God," a loving and caring God who does not judge people based on their sin, failures, and problems; a God who never gives up on humanity. These pastors are unique and are clearly distinguishable from social workers. They express their theological anthropology rather quickly, or in other words, in the way they speak about the people and their actions that follow. So, the credibility of the pastors is vital. They give a testimony of the hope that is in them to those with whom they minister precisely by letting them go, blessing them, and connecting them to others.

References

Baart, A. 2001. *Theorie van de presentie.* Utrecht.

Bons-Storm, Riet. 1989. *Hoe gaat het met jou? Pastoraat als komen tot verstaan.* Kampen: Kok.

Bruin, D., C. Meijerman, and H. Verbraeck. 2003. *Zwerven in de 21ste eeuw. Een exploratief onderzoek naar geestelijke gezondheidsproblematiek en overlast van dak — en thuislozen in Nederland.* Utrecht: Centrum voor Verslavingsonderzoek.

Daklozenmonitor 2006-2007, Gemeente Rotterdam 2007.

Davelaar, M., T. Nederland, M. Wentink, and S. Ter Woerds. 2006. *Aan de slag in de rafelrand. Werk en activering voor daklozen en verslaafden.* Verweij Jonker Instituut, 2e druk.

Dorp, Hermen van. 2005. *Drugs — en straatpastoraat. Presentie voor "heel de mens."* Utrecht: Kerkinactie.

Dijk, Bernadette van. 2010. "Zegen. Praktische beschrijving van mijn identiteit als straatpastor," in *Handelingen: Tijdschrift voor praktische theologie* 1.

Ganzevoort, R. 2007. *Zorg voor het verhaal.* Zoetermeer.

Jaarverslag Leger des Heils, 2007.

Voortgangsrapportage maatschappelijke opvang 2008, Ministerie VWS.

Index